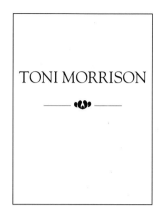

TONI MORRISON

TONI MORRISON

❧

Douglas Century

CHELSEA HOUSE PUBLISHERS
New York Philadelphia

Chelsea House Publishers
Editorial Director Richard Rennert
Executive Managing Editor Karyn Gullen Browne
Copy Chief Robin James
Picture Editor Adrian G. Allen
Art Director Robert Mitchell
Manufacturing Director Gerald Levine
Production Coordinator Marie Claire Cebrián-Ume

Black Americans of Achievement
Senior Editor Sean Dolan

Staff for TONI MORRISON
Editorial Assistants Annie McDonnell, Joy Sanchez
Designer John Infantino
Picture Researcher Lisa Kirchner
Cover Illustrator Janet Hamlin

3 5 7 9 8 6 4

Library of Congress Cataloging-in-Publication Data
Century, Douglas.
   Toni Morrison/Douglas Century.
      p. cm.—(Black Americans of achievement)
   Includes bibliographical references and index.
   ISBN 0-7910-1877-6.
   ISBN 0-7910-1906-3 (pbk.)
   1. Morrison, Toni—Biography—Juvenile literature. 2. Afro-
American women novelists—20th century—Biography—Juvenile
literature. [1. Morrison, Toni. 2. Authors, American. 3. Afro-
Americans—Biography.] I. Title. II. Series.
PS3563.08749Z6 1994   93-31166
813'.54—dc20   CIP
[B]   AC

Frontispiece: *Toni Morrison on the
campus of the State University of New
York at Albany, where she taught in
the mid-1980s.*

CONTENTS

On Achievement   8
Coretta Scott King

1
"Those People Were Me"   11

2
Life in Lorain   21

3
Howard and Beyond   31

4
"I Fell in Love with Myself"   41

5
Song of Toni   53

6
Lickety-Split, Lickety-Split   63

7
Dreaming Beloved   71

8
Jazz Age   83

Appendix: Books by Toni Morrison   97

Chronology   98

Further Reading   100

Index   101

BLACK AMERICANS OF ACHIEVEMENT

HENRY AARON
baseball great

KAREEM ABDUL-JABBAR
basketball great

RALPH ABERNATHY
civil rights leader

ALVIN AILEY
choreographer

MUHAMMAD ALI
heavyweight champion

RICHARD ALLEN
religious leader and
social activist

MAYA ANGELOU
author

LOUIS ARMSTRONG
musician

ARTHUR ASHE
tennis great

JOSEPHINE BAKER
entertainer

JAMES BALDWIN
author

BENJAMIN BANNEKER
scientist and mathematician

AMIRI BARAKA
poet and playwright

COUNT BASIE
bandleader and composer

ROMARE BEARDEN
artist

JAMES BECKWOURTH
frontiersman

MARY MCLEOD BETHUNE
educator

JULIAN BOND
civil rights leader and politician

GWENDOLYN BROOKS
poet

JIM BROWN
football great

RALPH BUNCHE
diplomat

STOKELY CARMICHAEL
civil rights leader

GEORGE WASHINGTON CARVER
botanist

RAY CHARLES
musician

CHARLES CHESNUTT
author

JOHN COLTRANE
musician

BILL COSBY
entertainer

PAUL CUFFE
merchant and abolitionist

COUNTEE CULLEN
poet

BENJAMIN DAVIS, SR., AND BENJAMIN DAVIS, JR.
military leaders

SAMMY DAVIS, JR.
entertainer

FATHER DIVINE
religious leader

FREDERICK DOUGLASS
abolitionist editor

CHARLES DREW
physician

W. E. B. DU BOIS
scholar and activist

PAUL LAURENCE DUNBAR
poet

KATHERINE DUNHAM
dancer and choreographer

DUKE ELLINGTON
bandleader and composer

RALPH ELLISON
author

JULIUS ERVING
basketball great

JAMES FARMER
civil rights leader

ELLA FITZGERALD
singer

MARCUS GARVEY
black nationalist leader

JOSH GIBSON
baseball great

DIZZY GILLESPIE
musician

WHOOPI GOLDBERG
entertainer

ALEX HALEY
author

PRINCE HALL
social reformer

MATTHEW HENSON
explorer

CHESTER HIMES
author

BILLIE HOLIDAY
singer

LENA HORNE
entertainer

LANGSTON HUGHES
poet

ZORA NEALE HURSTON
author

JESSE JACKSON
civil rights leader and politician

MICHAEL JACKSON
entertainer

JACK JOHNSON
heavyweight champion

JAMES WELDON JOHNSON
author

MAGIC JOHNSON
basketball great

SCOTT JOPLIN
composer

BARBARA JORDAN
politician

MICHAEL JORDAN
basketball great

CORETTA SCOTT KING
civil rights leader

MARTIN LUTHER KING, JR.
civil rights leader

LEWIS LATIMER
scientist

SPIKE LEE
filmmaker

CARL LEWIS
champion athlete

JOE LOUIS
heavyweight champion

RONALD MCNAIR
astronaut

MALCOLM X
militant black leader

THURGOOD MARSHALL
Supreme Court justice

TONI MORRISON
author

ELIJAH MUHAMMAD
religious leader

EDDIE MURPHY
entertainer

JESSE OWENS
champion athlete

SATCHEL PAIGE
baseball great

CHARLIE PARKER
musician

GORDON PARKS
photographer

ROSA PARKS
civil rights leader

SIDNEY POITIER
actor

ADAM CLAYTON
POWELL, JR.
political leader

COLIN POWELL
military leader

LEONTYNE PRICE
opera singer

A. PHILIP RANDOLPH
labor leader

PAUL ROBESON
singer and actor

JACKIE ROBINSON
baseball great

DIANA ROSS
entertainer

BILL RUSSELL
basketball great

JOHN RUSSWURM
publisher

SOJOURNER TRUTH
antislavery activist

HARRIET TUBMAN
antislavery activist

NAT TURNER
slave revolt leader

DENMARK VESEY
slave revolt leader

ALICE WALKER
author

MADAM C. J. WALKER
entrepreneur

BOOKER T. WASHINGTON
educator and racial spokesman

IDA WELLS-BARNETT
civil rights leader

WALTER WHITE
civil rights leader

OPRAH WINFREY
entertainer

STEVIE WONDER
musician

RICHARD WRIGHT
author

ON
ACHIEVEMENT

Coretta Scott King

BﾠEFORE YOU BEGIN this book, I hope you will ask yourself what the word *excellence* means to you. I think that it's a question we should all ask, and keep asking as we grow older and change. Because the truest answer to it should never change. When you think of excellence, perhaps you think of success at work; or of becoming wealthy; or meeting the right person, getting married, and having a good family life.

Those important goals are worth striving for, but there is a better way to look at excellence. As Martin Luther King, Jr., said in one of his last sermons, "I want you to be first in love. I want you to be first in moral excellence. I want you to be first in generosity. If you want to be important, wonderful. If you want to be great, wonderful. But recognize that he who is greatest among you shall be your servant."

My husband, Martin Luther King, Jr., knew that the true meaning of achievement is service. When I met him, in 1952, he was already ordained as a Baptist preacher and was working toward a doctoral degree at Boston University. I was studying at the New England Conservatory and dreamed of accomplishments in music. We married a year later, and after I graduated the following year we moved to Montgomery, Alabama. We didn't know it then, but our notions of achievement were about to undergo a dramatic change.

You may have read or heard about what happened next. What began with the boycott of a local bus line grew into a national movement, and by the time he was assassinated in 1968 my husband had fashioned a black movement powerful enough to shatter forever the practice of racial segregation. What you may not have read about is where he got his method for resisting injustice without compromising his religious beliefs.

He adopted the strategy of nonviolence from a man of a different race, who lived in a different country, and even practiced a different religion. The man was Mahatma Gandhi, the great leader of India, who devoted his life to serving humanity in the spirit of love and nonviolence. It was in these principles that Martin discovered his method for social reform. More than anything else, those two principles were the key to his achievements.

This book is about black Americans who served society through the excellence of their achievements. It forms a part of the rich history of black men and women in America—a history of stunning accomplishments in every field of human endeavor, from literature and art to science, industry, education, diplomacy, athletics, jurisprudence, even polar exploration.

Not all of the people in this history had the same ideals, but I think you will find something that all of them had in common. Like Martin Luther King, Jr., they all decided to become "drum majors" and serve humanity. In that principle—whether it was expressed in books, inventions, or song—they found something outside themselves to use as a goal and a guide. Something that showed them a way to serve others, instead of only living for themselves.

Reading the stories of these courageous men and women not only helps us discover the principles that we will use to guide our own lives but also teaches us about our black heritage and about America itself. It is crucial for us to know the heroes and heroines of our history and to realize that the price we paid in our struggle for equality in America was dear. But we must also understand that we have gotten as far as we have partly because America's democratic system and ideals made it possible.

We are still struggling with racism and prejudice. But the great men and women in this series are a tribute to the spirit of our democratic ideals and the system in which they have flourished. And that makes their stories special and worth knowing. ☙

1

"THOSE PEOPLE WERE ME"

I T WAS ANOTHER cold winter night in Syracuse, New York. The dishes were washed and the little boys were fast asleep in the next room. Outside a fierce wind was howling, kicking clouds of snowflakes up against the frosted windowpane. As she had done every night that winter, Toni Morrison, a young divorced mother of two, sat down at her writing desk to work on the story of the little black girl who wished for blue eyes.

That winter was one of the loneliest times of Morrison's life. Just divorced from her husband, she had moved to Syracuse with her two young sons to work as an associate editor at L. W. Singer, a textbook publishing subsidiary of Random House. But Morrison had a feeling she would not be staying long in Syracuse. She knew that in perhaps a year or two she would be transferred to New York City, and the idea of trying to make new friends in Syracuse was something she resisted.

Working from nine to five, trying to care for her little sons, and having very little social life, Morrison found herself growing increasingly depressed. In the mornings, she would leave little Harold and Slade with the housekeeper while she went off to her work at the publishing company. After work, like millions of working mothers across America, she would pre-

Toni Morrison addresses an audience of college students. The Nobel Prize for Literature she won in 1993 marked Morrison as the most important African-American writer and confirmed, as have her six novels to date, her oft-stated belief that "if you study the culture and art of African-Americans, you are not studying a regional or minor culture. What you are studying is America."

pare dinner for her sons and spend a few hours visiting with them until their bedtime.

And, then, at nine o'clock each night, when the boys were asleep and the house was very still, she would sit down with her notebooks and her pack of cigarettes and begin to write. As the words flowed from her pen, as she conjured up images and memories of her midwestern childhood, as the characters she was inventing began to take on personalities of their own, Morrison came to realize that writing could serve as a way to escape the feelings of loneliness and depression she felt in this strange, cold city.

As a girl growing up in the industrial town of Lorain, Ohio, Morrison had never really wanted to be a writer. She had always daydreamed about being a dancer. Later, as a student at Howard University in Washington, D.C., she had been known on campus as an actress; after college she had found herself working as an English teacher. And although she had always loved to read novels as a girl, and although teachers had often encouraged her to write, it was never anything she had seen herself doing with her life.

But several years earlier, when she and her husband were still living together in Washington, Morrison had joined a small group of poets and writers who met once a month to discuss each other's writing. For Morrison, it was more of a social outing than anything else. There was good food and good company at each meeting. Each writer was supposed to bring a story or poem to be critiqued by the others. For the first few sessions, Morrison simply dug up old things she had written in high school and brought them in. Then one day she didn't have any more "old junk" left to bring in, so she sat down to write something new.

It was then that she remembered something very strange and sad that had happened to her as a girl in

Ohio. She remembered having a conversation with another little black girl who said she had stopped believing in God because, after two years of praying for blue eyes, God still had not given them to her.

It was 1962, the early years of the civil rights movement, and Morrison immediately realized that this episode from her childhood said something profound about the way black children are taught to think about their identities at a very early age.

With little Harold Ford—then a toddler—crawling all over her lap, Morrison managed to quickly write out the story of the little girl who wished for blue eyes. She read the story to the writers' group, many of the members liked it, and then, thinking that the story was finished for good, she put it away in her drawer and all but forgot about it.

Five years later, during that cold Syracuse winter of 1967, Morrison rediscovered the story and began to fashion it into her first novel, *The Bluest Eye*. The novel would be remarkable for the power of its language and the brutal vision it presented of three young black girls coming of age in postdepression Ohio.

Morrison would later say that in writing *The Bluest Eye* she was attempting to craft the kind of book she herself wanted to read, the kind of book she did not see being published in America, a book that presented "the people who in all literature were always peripheral—little black girls who were props, background; those people were never center stage, and those people were me."

The books Morrison had read by black American writers to that point were largely written by men: Richard Wright, Ralph Ellison, James Baldwin. And while these men were undoubtedly very powerful writers, writers of genius, something about the tone of their prose left Morrison cold. It seemed as if they were always addressing themselves to a white audience, making a case to their white readers, explaining things about black culture that Morrison knew they would not have to explain to her if they were sitting across the table from her sharing a pot of coffee.

Morrison wanted to write a book about black people, in the language of black people, without having to explain the nuances of her world to her white readers. And she was unapologetic about this idea of writing first and foremost for a black readership. "I never asked Tolstoy to write for me, a little colored girl in Lorain, Ohio," she would reflect, years later. "I never asked Joyce not to mention Catholicism or the world of Dublin."

"Quiet as it's kept, there were no marigolds in the fall of 1941," begins the narration of Morrison's novel, and even with this choice of words, she makes a statement about the audience she means to address.

"If I say 'Quiet as it's kept,'" she would later tell a magazine interviewer, "that is a piece of information which means exactly what it says, but to black people it means a big lie is about to be told. Or someone is going to tell some graveyard information, who's sleeping with whom. Black readers will chuckle."

That winter of 1967, thoughts of the civil rights movement seemed always to be on Morrison's mind. Martin Luther King, Jr., and his colleagues were spearheading an effort to desegregate the South. And one of Morrison's students during her teaching days at Howard University, Stokely Carmichael, was gaining recognition as a leader of the Student Nonviolent Coordinating Committee (SNCC).

But with all the talk of "Black Power" spreading across the country, Morrison felt that something fundamentally important was not being addressed. "Whatever was going on, was not about me," she would remember, years later. "There were lots of noises being made about how wonderful I was—'black

*Richard Wright, seen here
in the study of his Brooklyn
home, is generally regarded as
the most important African-
American novelist before
Morrison. Wright's seminal novel
Native Son was published in
1940 and tells the disturbing story
of Bigger Thomas, a young black
inhabitant of the Chicago ghetto
whose circumstances propel him to
two murders. "The birth of the
modern Afro-American novel is
marked by the publication of
Richard Wright's Native Son in
1940," wrote the editors of the
Encyclopedia of Black America
in 1981.*

woman, you are my queen.' I didn't believe it. . . .
Nobody was going to tell me that it had been that
easy. That all I needed was a slogan: 'Black is
Beautiful.' It wasn't that easy being a little black girl
in this country—it was rough. The psychological
tricks you have to play in order to get through—and
nobody said how it felt to be that."

Although there had been notable black women
writers before her—Zora Neale Hurston, Lorraine
Hansberry, Gwendolyn Brooks—they were not being
widely read or taught in the universities in the

mid-1960s, and Morrison did not feel their influence much on her writing. Setting out to write *The Bluest Eye*, Morrison really felt she was alone in trying to capture on paper the world of the black characters she saw in her mind, that the burden was on her alone to tell the stories of these people, that there was no one else in America who was attempting to do justice to "this complex poetic life . . . as grand and as intricate and as profound as [that of] anybody who had walked this earth."

The Bluest Eye tells the story of three black schoolgirls growing up in Lorain, Ohio, the sisters Claudia and Frieda McTeer and their friend Pecola Breedlove. While Claudia and Frieda live in the home of strict, protective parents, Pecola Breedlove is a very unhappy child, ignored by her mother and abused by her father.

Claudia, who relates much of the story in her own voice, is a strong-willed eight-year-old black girl who cannot stand the sight of little blond-haired dolls with blue eyes; when one is given to her for Christmas she tears it to pieces, plucking out the eyes and pulling apart the limbs. Claudia also hates the sight of the child movie star Shirley Temple, with her flowing golden curls and baby-blue eyes. Not because everyone said Shirley Temple was cute, but because Shirley Temple got to dance in the movies with Bill "Bojangles" Robinson, the legendary black tap-dancing star, who Claudia feels "ought to have been soft-shoeing it and chuckling" with her instead.

Eleven-year-old Pecola Breedlove, on the other hand, seems to love Shirley Temple. She is always asking to drink milk out of Claudia's blue-and-white Shirley Temple cup. Pecola is a very lonely girl. Her classmates tease her constantly. They tell her she is ugly. They singsong at her that her father is a drunk and that he sleeps naked in the living room. Claudia and Frieda McTeer are Pecola's only friends.

The author James Baldwin as a young expatriate in Paris, France. The most prominent African-American writer of the literary generation between Wright and Morrison, Baldwin was a great admirer of Morrison's work. Shortly before his death in 1987, he said that her recently published masterpiece, the novel Beloved, *"could be about the story of truth," and he described Morrison as "this rather elegant matron, whose intentions really are serious, and according to some people, lethal."*

And though much of *The Bluest Eye* is written from the children's point of view, the subject matter touches on some very adult themes. Pecola, the sad little girl who thinks everything in her life would be all right if only she could have blue eyes, is raped by her drunken father and becomes pregnant with his child. As her pregnancy begins to show, Pecola's mother beats her terribly and she must stop going to school with the other children. When the baby is born prematurely and dies, Pecola begins to go mad. Desperate and confused, she visits a West Indian preacher called Soaphead Church to see if he can give her the blue eyes she has always wanted. Soap-head Church, an unscrupulous and mean-spirited man, leads Pecola to believe that God will give her blue eyes, but that she will be the only one who can see them. By the end of the book, Pecola is left talking to an imaginary friend, asking over and over if her eyes are indeed the bluest eyes of all.

Writing *The Bluest Eye,* Morrison often worked late into the night. Sometimes she would stop writing, gaze out the window at the snowdrifts that had banked up high against the fences, and think back to the cold winters she had known as a girl in Ohio. Occasionally, six-month-old Slade would begin to cry in the next room and she would have to go in and pacify him. She could never tell her children not to disturb her while she was writing. She knew that two little boys had little use for a late-night writer in the house; what they needed was a full-time mother.

In those days, Morrison wrote only for herself. She did not think much about whether or not the book would be published. Sometimes she would think, "No one is ever going to read this until I'm dead." She wasn't sure she would ever write another novel—perhaps a play or a short story someday. But whether *The Bluest Eye* was published or not, Morrison knew one thing: she was already committed to a life of writing.

After receiving many rejection letters telling her that her book had "no beginning, no middle, and no end" or that her "writing [was] wonderful, but . . . ," the manuscript of Morrison's novel was finally accepted for publication by a young editor at Holt, Rinehart & Winston. By the time *The Bluest Eye* was published in 1970, Morrison and her two young sons had moved to New York City, where she was now working as a senior editor for Random House.

The book did not sell especially well, but it did receive appreciative reviews by book critics across the country. John Leonard, in the *New York Times*, would single out Morrison for writing "a prose so precise, so faithful to speech and so charged with pain and wonder that the novel becomes poetry." And Liz Gant, writing for *Black World*, would praise Morrison for having the courage to address "an aspect of the Black experience that many of us would rather forget, our hatred of ourselves."

What neither the critics, nor even Morrison herself, could know back then was that the publication of *The Bluest Eye* had begun the career of one of the 20th century's most influential novelists—the first African-American writer to win the Nobel Prize in Literature.

Years of celebrity and critical acclaim lay ahead. But for Morrison, the healing process of writing she had discovered during those lonely winter months in Syracuse would always remain the most intimate and personal of experiences. Years later she would remark that if all the publishers in the world were to disappear, she would continue to write anyway.

"Writing for me was the most extraordinary way of thinking and feeling," she would say. "It became the one thing I was doing that I had absolutely no intention of living without." ❧

2

LIFE IN LORAIN

A CHILD OF the Great Depression, the woman who would one day be known as Toni Morrison was born on February 18, 1931, in the steel-mill town of Lorain, Ohio. Her father, George Wofford, was a shipyard welder who had come to Ohio from Georgia; her mother, Ramah Willis Wofford, had migrated north from Alabama. They christened their second daughter Chloe Anthony Wofford.

Both the Wofford and the Willis families, like many Southern blacks in the early years of the century, had fled the South's virulent and institutionalized racism in search of better educational and employment opportunities in the North.

Toni Morrison's maternal grandfather, John Solomon Willis, was an ex-slave who had once owned 88 acres of land in Greenville, Alabama. When unscrupulous white Southerners cheated him out of his property, the Willis family embarked upon the long trek northward. They arrived in Ohio by way of Kentucky, where John Solomon Willis, a carpenter by trade, worked in the coal mines for a time.

"My grandmother did washing, and my mother and her sister went to a little one-room school," Toni Morrison would tell *Newsweek* magazine years later. "One day the teacher, who was about 16 and white, was doing long division and having trouble explaining it. Since my mother and her sister already knew long division, they explained it to her and the class. They came home all excited and proud of themselves, crowing, 'Mama, guess

The officers of the senior class of 1949 at Lorain High School in Lorain, Ohio. Chloe Wofford (standing, at far left), who would later be known to the world as Toni Morrison, was the senior class treasurer.

Downtown Lorain in 1927, four years before Morrison was born there. Twenty-five miles west of Cleveland, on Lake Erie, Lorain is a small industrial city whose economy in the 20th century has been dependent on steel mills, shipbuilding, railroad shops, motor vehicle assembly plants, and the production of construction equipment.

what we did? We taught the teacher long division!' My grandmother just said to her husband, 'Come on, Johnny, we have to move.'"

The Willis family finally settled in Lorain, a small industrial community on the shores of Lake Erie, about 25 miles west of Cleveland. It was a town of newcomers, full of immigrant Europeans and Mexicans and Southern blacks, all of whom had come to Ohio seeking work in the steel mills.

Ohio was, in many respects, a very divided state. The northern part of the state had a long history of abolitionism, and bordering on Canada to the north, had been a vital route in the so-called Underground Railroad of slaves escaping to freedom. Oberlin, a town only 13 miles away from Lorain, had been an important stop on the Underground Railroad, and its renowned college had admitted blacks and women in the 19th century, long before any other university in the country.

The southern part of Ohio, however, was vastly different. Bordering on Kentucky, it had a more Southern character and was long a haven for the Ku Klux Klan. Cross burnings and racist violence were not uncommon in this part of the state. During slavery, crossing over the Ohio River had often represented the escape to freedom for runaway slaves, but Ohio was by no means a perfect sanctuary.

"Ohio is a curious juxtaposition of what was ideal in this country and what was base," Toni Morrison would recall. "It was also a Mecca for black people; they came to the mills and plants because Ohio offered the possibility of a good life, the possibility of freedom, even though there were some terrible obstacles. Ohio also offers an escape from stereotyped black settings. It is neither plantation nor ghetto."

George Wofford, Toni Morrison's father, was a dignified and industrious man who, for almost 17 years while his children were young, somehow managed to hold down three jobs simultaneously. Throughout the deprivations of the Great Depression, he managed to wear expensive Florsheim shoes and natty clothes. As a shipyard welder, he took such pride in his work that he would weld his name into the sides of the ships on which he worked whenever he saw that he'd welded a perfect seam.

The period of George Wofford's upbringing in Georgia was one of the most murderous times in American history. Lynchings of young black men reached epidemic proportions—between the years 1882 and 1925 there were an estimated 3,783 lynchings in the United States, the vast majority of the victims being young black males. The vicious brand of racism he had seen and experienced as a boy in the South left George Wofford with a deep distrust for all white people, so much so that Toni Morrison would not hesitate, years later, to label her own father a racist.

"People assume that a racist is a white person that doesn't like black people," she would say, "but the term simply means a person who believes that his race is superior to another race. My father in that sense really felt that all black people were better than all white people because their position was [inherently] a moral one."

George Wofford would tell his children that "there could never be any harmony between the races" because white people were "genetically corrupt," and therefore

The more literarily inclined students at Lorain High School often worked in the school library as aides. Among the library aides in the class of 1949 was Chloe Wofford (second from left in the first row).

fundamentally incapable of transcending the bigotry they had learned from an early age. And he would constantly remind young Chloe—she would not start calling herself Toni until years later, at college—that "where he came from, Georgia, was populated by the detritus of Europe and it was difficult for them to be any better than what they were."

But Chloe's mother was not persuaded by her husband's line of reasoning. Ramah Wofford had a much more optimistic view of race relations, feeling that even people who had grown up in a prejudiced society could be improved through proper education. And Chloe tended to agree with her mother; she would listen to her father's tirades about the evils of the white man, but deep down she knew he was wrong.

"I went to school with white children—they were my friends. There was no awe, no fear," she would say of the time. "Only later, when things got . . . sexual . . . did I see how clear the lines really were. But when I was in first grade nobody thought I was inferior. I was the only black in the class and the only child who could read!"

One of the more memorable episodes of Chloe's childhood involved a physical confrontation between her father and a white man who had followed Chloe and her older sister into their apartment building.

Today, no one seems sure if the white man had any kind of hostile intentions toward the Wofford girls, or if he was simply an innocent bystander who became the victim of George Wofford's hot and sometimes overprotective temper.

"I do remember a white man following my sister and me into our house, up the stairs," Morrison recollected during a 1983 interview on German radio. "We lived in an apartment on the second floor. My father was there, and he picked up [the white man] and threw him down the stairs, and then picked up our tricycle and threw the tricycle down after him. My father was not a tall man and this man loomed large. All he knew was that this man was behind his girls, and he was, you know, defending his household."

The episode left a distinct impression on the future novelist. "I had not seen abusive, physically abusive white people as many people have in the United States, so the first racial encounter I had as a child was one in which my father was triumphant, physically triumphant, and it's important that what I first saw was that kind of assertion on the part of my father."

Chloe's father also instilled in his sons and daughters his unwavering sense of self-respect. At the age of 13 Chloe got a job cleaning the house of a white family after school. One day she came to her father complaining that the work was too hard and that the woman was mean to her. "Girl, you don't live there," he told her. "You live here. So you go do your work, get your money and come on home."

There were no exclusively black neighborhoods in depression-era Lorain, and throughout Chloe's childhood the Woffords lived in close proximity to white people, mostly European immigrants. Their next-door neighbors on one side were a Greek family and on the other an Italian family.

Although the town did not have any of the formal or legal segregation of the South—"it was too small,

Wofford's yearbook photo as a senior at Lorain High. She took part in far more school activities than most of her classmates, including school aid, music, the Senate Council, the yearbook, the drama club, and the National Honor Society.

Wofford at work (foreground) as an associate editor for the Hi-Standard, the Lorain High School yearbook.

too poor, to have officially racist structures," Toni Morrison would later remember—there were places that were unofficially off-limits to black people.

One of those places was Lake Erie, in which the black residents of Lorain were prohibited from swimming. "They had one park where the lake was accessible and we weren't permitted to go there," remembered Morrison, "and so we went further up the shore to a place that was wilderness which the black people had made into their own park, so to speak."

Despite its intimate mix of Europeans, Latinos, and African Americans, Lorain was no "happy melting pot,—but at least it was possible in Ohio, unlike the South, to take legal action if you felt you had been discriminated against." Chloe's uncles were constantly bringing lawsuits against "people who refused to serve you in ice-cream parlors" and other similar forms of business-related bias.

And unlike Chloe's quite demonstrative father, Ramah Wofford—a churchgoing woman who sang in the choir—was engaged in more subtle protests against the town's racial discrimination. "My mother's great thing was to go into a theatre—they had a habit of putting all black people into one part of the theatre," Morrison remembered, "and so she would make it her business to go in there on Saturday afternoon and sit where she wished."

Once, during the Great Depression, the Wofford family received some government-relief food that was infested with bugs; Chloe's mother did not hesitate to write a long letter of protest to the president of the United States, Franklin Delano Roosevelt.

As a second child and a second daughter—the two children that followed her being boys—Chloe felt as if she was in the "most anonymous position in the world." Like many introspective children, she very early on became engrossed in books and stories. She entered the first grade already knowing how to read, and by the time she was an adolescent she was poring over volumes of the masterpieces of European literature. She especially loved the great Russian novelists, Dostoevski and Tolstoy, but she also read *Madame Bovary*, by the French writer Gustave Flaubert, and the novels of the 19th-century English writer Jane Austen.

"Those books were not written for a little black girl in Lorain, Ohio," she would reflect years later, "but they were so magnificently done that I got them anyway— they spoke directly to me out of their own specificity."

Although Chloe had still never considered becoming a writer—she dreamed of being a dancer like the famous ballerina, Maria Tallchief—those great Russian, French, and English novels had a tremendous impact on her imagination. When the time came years later for Toni Morrison to put her own pen to paper in *The Bluest Eye*, her first novel, she set out to "capture that same specificity about the nature and feeling of the culture I grew up in" as Dostoevski had done for his Russian characters or Jane Austen had done for the English.

But young Chloe's imagination was also shaped by a tradition much closer to home, a tradition she inherited through both her mother's and father's side of

Wofford (third from left, middle row) as a member of the Lorain High School Student Council.

the family—the rich legacy of Southern black folklore and mythology. Throughout her childhood she absorbed the folktales, fables, and songs that for centuries had been such an important aspect of Southern black culture. Ramah Wofford had a beautiful voice and Chloe would constantly hear her mother singing melodies she had learned as a girl in Mississippi. One children's song which the Willis family sang in Mississippi began with the words "Green, the only son of Solomon," and it was a song that would later be used by Toni Morrison in one of her most famous novels.

There was always a lot of storytelling in the Wofford home. Chloe's mother and father would spend hours telling the children thrilling and often terrifying ghost stories. "We were intimate with the supernatural," Morrison would later recall. Chloe's grandmother recorded her dreams in a book and would decode the symbols in her nightly dreams in order to know which number to bet on when she played the numbers.

At Lorain High School Chloe was an excellent student, learning Latin and graduating with honors. Her mother was a high school graduate but her father was not, and only one relative in her entire family had attended college. Nevertheless, Chloe was determined to further her education. She applied to and was accepted by Howard University in Washington, D.C., one of the nation's oldest and most prestigious black colleges.

Leaving Lorain for college at the tender age of 17, Chloe Wofford would look back on life in her hometown and think it must surely have been the single most boring place to grow up in the entire world.

But in later years she would come to realize otherwise. She would recognize that her upbringing in the racially and ethnically diverse town had exposed her to a number of elements that were so typically American and had given her a breadth of understanding that would be invaluable to her career as a novelist.

"There's some places you can be born where you're really very sheltered," she would tell an interviewer in later years. "And I didn't have that luxury—which would have crippled me I think." Growing up in the heart of the country, in the great Midwest, would prove to be an invaluable learning experience for the future writer, allowing Chloe Anthony Wofford the opportunity to become "intimately acquainted with all those forces that are American," preparing her for whatever obstacles she might encounter as she said good-bye to life in Lorain and departed for her years of college in the nation's capital. ❧

3

HOWARD AND BEYOND

FOUNDED IN 1867 by the First Congregational Society, an organization of white clergymen, the Howard Normal and Theological Institute of Teachers and Preachers quickly expanded beyond its stated goal of providing "an institution for training (colored) preachers with a view to service among the freedmen." Named for General Oliver Otis Howard, a white Civil War hero who was the commissioner of the Freedmen's Bureau, a government agency established to assist freed slaves, Howard University would soon become the jewel of the nation's black colleges, an elite institution often referred to as the "capstone of Negro education."

Howard would be home to such legendary black educators as Alain Locke, the philosopher and critic who was the godfather of the so-called Harlem Renaissance movement of the 1920s, and Sterling A. Brown, the poet and professor of literature who helped to establish African-American literary criticism. Among the university's more prominent graduates were former Supreme Court justice Thurgood Marshall and Virginia governor L. Douglas Wilder, as well as opera singer Jessye Norman and actor Ossie Davis. The campus was also the center of black collegiate social life; many of the country's black fraternities and sororities were founded at Howard.

31

Members of the Alpha Kappa Alpha sorority, to which Morrison belonged, on the Howard campus in 1949. Morrison was somewhat disillusioned by the emphasis on social life she found at Howard.

Like many young people who come to prestigious universities wide-eyed and full of expectation, Chloe Wofford was more than a little disappointed once she adjusted to the reality of life on Howard's sprawling 130-acre campus in northwest Washington, D.C. Fresh out of working-class Lorain, Ohio, she was not prepared for the middle-class values she found at Howard. To Chloe, who so loved reading and literature, the student life at Howard seemed to revolve more around socializing than serious study. "It was about getting married, buying clothes, and going to parties," she would later say. "Boys chose their sweethearts on their color, the straightness of their hair, their father's money. I was astonished."

One episode which stuck in Chloe's mind, and which seemed representative of the shallowness of the social life she found in college, involved a tall, dark-skinned girl who none of the "cool" guys on campus wanted to have much to do with.

"She was the straight man to the pretty girls. I liked her a lot, but she had no dates, and wasn't popular. She didn't care, she had a boy back home whom she liked and eventually married. But during her senior year, her parents came to visit her. They turned out to be very wealthy, and, good God, she was overwhelmed. Suddenly all the dudes on campus, in their white jackets with their stethoscopes dangling out of their pockets, started coming around. They had a rush on that poor girl for the last six months."

Since many people at Howard had problems pronouncing her first name correctly, Chloe shortened her middle name—Anthony—and began calling herself "Toni." Although she disapproved of the heavy emphasis Howard placed on such superficial qualities as the lightness of one's skin—certain sororities would not accept girls who were darker than a given shade—Toni survived her undergraduate years by being, in her own words, "jolly and fun."

Toni majored in English, minored in classics, and was a student of the pioneering African-American literature professor Sterling Brown. Black literary consciousness was little known in the late 1940s, and even at a black college like Howard, great African-American writers such as Langston Hughes, Zora Neale Hurston, and Jean Toomer were not read. In one of her classes Toni proposed that she present a term paper on the black characters in Shakespeare, but her professor seemed "horrified" by the idea, telling her that this was not an appropriate subject for literary study. There was one aspect of college life that really held some attraction for Toni, the one place where she felt "hard work, thought, and talent was praised": it was in the campus theatrical company, the Howard University Players. Toni joined the repertory company, made up of students and faculty, and with the Howard Players made several tours of the Deep South, "seeing its roads, its shotgun houses, its schools, its particular brand of segregation." Segregation was not something Toni was completely

The Howard Players, seen here costumed for a production of Shakespeare's The Merry Wives of Windsor, *were one of the most distinguished university theater troupes in the country.*

unfamiliar with at this point; Washington, D.C., itself, although the nation's capital, was still a segregated Southern town in the late 1940s.

But it was on these tours of the Deep South with the Howard Players that Toni first came to understand the way of life in the region that had once been home to her own parents and grandparents. The Howard Players performed before audiences that were almost completely black, and Toni and her fellow actors and actresses had virtually no contact with white Southerners during their tours. Seeing first-hand what life was like for Southern blacks in the late 1940s and early 1950s made the stories Toni had heard as a girl from her father and mother about the hardships of life in the South seem more real, particularly the tale of injustice involving her grandfather John Solomon Willis, who had been cheated out of his 88 acres of Alabama land, land legally granted to his Indian mother by the U.S. government following the Civil War.

After graduating from Howard, Toni decided to further her study of literature by pursuing a master's degree in English at Cornell University. She still was not entertaining any ideas about becoming a writer, but thought she would go into teaching after graduate school. She completed her master's at Cornell in 1955, doing her graduate thesis on the theme of suicide in the novels of William Faulkner and Virginia Woolf.

From Cornell, Toni went on to Texas Southern University in Houston, where she was offered a position teaching introductory English. The time in Houston would prove an important one; Morrison would later recollect that it was at Texas Southern that she first began to develop a cultural and historical "consciousness of being black." Whereas the professors at Howard had seemed to discourage the study of black culture, at Texas Southern "they always had Negro history week," something Toni had never experienced growing up in the North. And it was in the year and a half she spent as a novice teacher in Houston that Toni first "began to think about black culture as a subject, as an idea, as a discipline. Before that it had only been on a very personal level—my family."

She returned to Howard University in late 1957, this time not as a student but as a member of the faculty. The civil rights movement was still in its earliest phases then; in Alabama in 1956, a young Dr. Martin Luther King, Jr., had successfully organized the Montgomery bus boycott, a nonviolent protest of that city's segregated bus system set in motion by Rosa Parks's refusal to give up her seat to a white passenger in December 1955.

Morrison as she appeared as a graduating senior in the 1953 Howard University yearbook. She went on to do graduate work at Cornell University and to teach at Texas Southern University before returning to Howard as a teacher.

Toni Wofford was keenly interested in the civil rights movement, and although she did not take an active role in the protests, during her years teaching English at Howard she would meet several young people who would go on to play key roles in the struggle for African-American equality. There was the fiery poet Amiri Baraka, then called LeRoi Jones, who, Morrison would remember, "really turned that campus around"; and there was Andrew Young, who would go on to work alongside Dr. King and later be elected mayor of Atlanta.

One of the more memorable students Toni taught in her English classes was a young man named Stokely Carmichael. "He was the kind of student you always want in a class," she would recall years later, "smart, perceptive, funny and a bit of a rogue. He never worked, and he stimulated all the others to think." Upon graduation, Morrison asked Carmichael what he was planning to do next; he told her he'd been accepted at the Union Theological Seminary in New York, but first he was going to spend the summer down in Mississippi. He never made it to the seminary. Very shortly after graduating from Howard, Stokely Carmichael would rise to national prominence as a leader of the Student Nonviolent Coordinating Committee (SNCC) and as one of the most vocal advocates of the Black Power movement.

Another of Toni Wofford's English students, a boy named Claude Brown, once came to her after class and asked her to read an 800-page manuscript he had written. Toni was shocked. "I said, what? Eight hundred pages? Claude, come on! A nickel a word I'll read it for you." Brown's manuscript would turn out to be one of the classics of 20th-century African-American literature, the memoir *Manchild in the Promised Land*, published in 1965.

While teaching at Howard, Toni Wofford met and fell in love with a young architect from Jamaica named Harold Morrison. They were married in 1958; and their first son, Harold Ford, was born in 1961.

Unfortunately, the marriage would not prove to be a happy one. Although Toni Morrison remains to this day extremely guarded about this period in her life, she has attributed the difficulties in her marriage in part to the cultural differences between herself and her Jamaican husband.

"Women in Jamaica are very subservient in their marriages," she would say in a 1979 interview with the *New York Times Magazine*. "They never challenge their husbands. I was a constant nuisance to mine. He didn't need me making judgments about him, which I did. A lot."

One of Morrison's most memorable students during her time as a teacher at Howard was Stokely Carmichael, seen here addressing university students in Tallahassee, Florida, in 1967. Carmichael rose to national prominence as the head of the Student Nonviolent Coordinating Committee, a civil rights organization, and as one of the advocates of the movement for black self-determination known as Black Power.

In later years she would look back on the period of her marriage as a time of extreme emptiness and confusion. "It was as though I had nothing left but my imagination. I had no will, no judgment, no perspective, no power, no authority, no self—just this brutal sense of irony, melancholy and a trembling respect for words."

During the six years of marriage, Toni Morrison continued to teach English at Howard, as well as take care of her husband and her son Harold Ford. Feeling slightly restless, she decided to join a small writers' group in Washington. The decision had less to do with being a writer, she realized, than with being a young married woman looking for a night of good company and stimulating conversation, a night out with people who were poets and writers and who cared as much about literature as she did.

Each member of the group was required to bring in a story or poem for discussion; one week, having nothing to bring in, Toni dashed off her little short story about a black girl who wished for blue eyes. She read it to the group, listened to their appreciative responses, and then filed the story away, thinking she was finished with it for good. For Toni, writing was still little more than an occasional evening hobby.

In 1964, pregnant with her second child, Toni Morrison left her position in the English department at Howard University and departed with her husband and son on a trip to Europe. By the time she returned from Europe, her marriage had "dissolved in smoke."

She was now a 34-year-old single mother with one child to care for and a second on the way. To make matters worse, she had no job lined up to support them. Unhappy and uncertain, she returned to the one place she knew she could always turn to for solace—her parents' home in Lorain, Ohio. ❧

4

"I FELL IN LOVE
WITH MYSELF"

WHEN SHE ACCEPTED the position of associate editor with a textbook subsidiary of Random House in Syracuse, New York, in the fall of 1964, Toni Morrison knew she was embarking on a new career in publishing, but she could not possibly have anticipated the direction that career would take.

Adjusting to life in Syracuse would prove difficult. Hoping to be transferred to Random House's main offices in New York City before too long, Morrison resisted "putting down roots" or making close friendships in Syracuse. Working all day long to develop school textbooks that addressed the African-American experience, with her sons left in the care of a housekeeper, Morrison would return home each night to cook dinner for her children and then put them to bed.

It was then, in the lonely hours when the house was still and her sons fast asleep, that Toni Morrison began to write in earnest.

She dug up the short story she had written in her Washington writers' group years earlier and decided to expand it into a novel. The story had been inspired in part by Morrison's childhood friendship with another little black girl who had spent two years wishing for blue eyes.

As she began working on the novel, Morrison was reminded of her own feelings growing up in Ohio,

"Writing was for me the most extraordinary way of thinking and feeling. It became the one thing I was doing that I had absolutely no intention of living without," Morrison said in 1972 about the beginning of her literary career.

and she summoned up many memories—both fond and bitter—of life in Lorain, her girlhood home.

It began as something mysterious, this fictional delving into the past. As she would later tell an interviewer, one of the main reasons someone begins to write fiction is that "there is something in the past that is haunting, that is not or wasn't clear, so that you are almost constantly rediscovering the past."

Although Morrison drew on many memories in writing her first novel, the tale that she told in *The Bluest Eye* was very much a work of her own imagination. Exploring the relationship of three little black girls growing up in depression-era Ohio, Morrison infused each of her characters with aspects of her own personality, and in so doing, she embarked on an extraordinary voyage of self-discovery, fashioning a powerful new identity for herself.

"All of those people were me," she would later tell the novelist Gloria Naylor, of the characters she was inventing. "I was Pecola, Claudia . . . I was everybody. And as I began to [write], I began to pick up scraps of things that I had seen or felt, or didn't see or didn't feel, but imagined. And speculated about and wondered about. And I fell in love with myself. I reclaimed myself and the world—a real revelation. I named it. I described it. I listed it. I identified it. I recreated it."

Working days as an editor, Morrison would return home each night to her writing desk, venturing further into this mysterious voyage of self-discovery. In those early days in Syracuse, though, writing was still something she did "privately at night, like women with families who use their off-hours for creative projects." She still didn't feel comfortable calling herself "a writer"—it was just something that gave her some enjoyment, something she did to "pass the time."

She didn't expect to achieve recognition doing it, either. Writing *The Bluest Eye*, Morrison was fully convinced that "no one is ever going to read this until I'm dead." But she realized that even if the book was never published, the act of writing had unlocked "a very special place" inside her, and her life would never be the same again.

"Once I began 'The Bluest Eye,' it was such an energizing experience," she would tell the *Chicago Tribune* years later. "I felt bored with what was out there."

Writing every night soon became "a way of life" for Morrison. She felt "so good and excited and challenged" as she worked on and finally finished the manuscript of *The Bluest Eye*. "Nothing except parenthood challenged me in that way," she would later recall. "Whether or not it was successful—or even whether or not it was published—I was already committed. Already."

The expected transfer to the main offices of Random House came soon enough. After only 18 months in Syracuse, Toni Morrison packed up little Harold and Slade and embarked upon a new life in New York City. She found a house in the borough of Queens and every day would commute by subway to her new job at Random House headquarters on East 50th Street in Manhattan.

Morrison began her career in New York as a senior literary editor in the textbook division, but soon moved to the more prestigious "trade" section, editing books by such prominent black Americans as Muhammad Ali, Andrew Young, and Angela Davis. She also helped to develop the careers of a number of other up-and-coming black women writers, including Toni Cade Bambara and Gayl Jones.

"Toni has done more to encourage and publish other black writers than anyone I know," Andrew Young would tell *Newsweek* magazine in 1981.

At Random House, Morrison edited numerous important books by black authors. Among the writers she worked with was the scholar and activist Angela Davis, who won notoriety in the late 1960s and early 1970s when she was dismissed from the University of California at Los Angeles for her political views and then falsely imprisoned on trumped-up criminal charges.

Meanwhile, there was her own literary career to consider. She had been sending out the manuscript of *The Bluest Eye* to numerous publishers—and been receiving numerous polite rejection letters, telling her things like "this book has no beginning, no middle, and no end."

Eventually, Morrison did find an editor at Holt, Rinehart & Winston who agreed to publish the novel.

Initially, the publication of *The Bluest Eye* in 1970 did not change Toni Morrison's everyday life in a dramatic way. The book was not a great commercial success, and she continued her full-time work as an editor at Random House. But the novel received a good deal of critical attention, most of which

Morrison also edited The Greatest, *the autobiography of heavyweight boxing champion Muhammad Ali, whose embrace of the Nation of Islam and refusal to fight in the Vietnam War made him one of the most controversial political figures of his day as well as one of its most accomplished athletes.*

was appreciative. Morrison was credited by Chikwenye Okonjo Ogunyemi in *Critique: Studies in Modern Fiction* with portraying "in poignant terms the tragic condition of blacks in a racist America." And Phyllis R. Klotman, writing in *Black American Literature Forum*, praised the novel's "lyrical yet precise" use of language.

With the appearance of *The Bluest Eye*, Toni Morrison also established herself as an authority on black cultural issues, and over the next few years she published many articles and book reviews, primarily for the *New York Times*.

For several months after she had finished writing *The Bluest Eye*, Morrison found herself in a bit of a panic. She didn't immediately have another idea for a book and she began to worry that she might never be inspired to write fiction again.

But then, during the early morning commute by subway into Manhattan, certain ideas began to run through her mind. Her first book had focused on the experiences of three little black girls growing up in an environment of racist discrimination. Now she started to imagine a relationship between two adult black women who had been friends since childhood. One of the women, Nel Wright, would be a fairly conventional person, wanting to get married, have children, and fit into society. But the other character would be a social outcast, someone who wanted to break all the rules.

That character, called Sula Peace, would prove to be one of the most remarkable—and challenging—of Toni Morrison's literary creations.

"Sula was hard for me," Morrison would tell an interviewer in later years; "[it was] very difficult to make up that kind of character. Not difficult to think it up, but difficult to describe a woman who could be used as a classic type of evil force. Other people could use her that way. And at the same time I didn't want to make her freakish or repulsive or unattractive."

Morrison decided to set the novel in a town called Medallion, Ohio, between the years 1919 and 1965. Unlike the locale of *The Bluest Eye*, for which she could draw on childhood memories of Lorain, the physical setting of *Sula* had to be wholly fabricated—although she did base one aspect of the novel on something her mother had told her about living in Pittsburgh in the early days of her marriage:

"I remember her telling me that in those days all the black people lived in the hills of Pittsburgh," she remembered, "but now they lived amid the smoke and dirt in the heart of that city. It's clear up in those hills, and so I used that idea, but in a small river town in Ohio."

In *Sula*, Morrison would attempt to do something that had rarely—if ever—been tried in American fiction: to intensely explore the relationship between two black women. It was the early 1970s, and the women's liberation movement was gaining momentum in the United States; but there was something that made Toni Morrison uneasy about what was then still a white-dominated, middle-class movement.

"The thrust was that we had to start loving one another, begin being sisters," she told a British newspaper, the *Independent*, years later. "And I thought: 'What do they mean, *begin?*' I remembered how my family had helped one another and their friends in the community. That friendship was powerful and it wasn't about men. *Sula* was created out of the feeling that the way black women related to one another was different from the way white women related."

The relationship between Nel Wright and Sula Peace is anything but conventional. Even as little girls, they are bound together by a powerful secret. One day when they are playing down by the river, Sula begins swinging a young boy named Chicken Little around in a circle; suddenly, he slips from her hands and flies into the water.

> The water darkened and closed quickly over the place where Chicken Little sank. The pressure of his hard and tight little fingers was still in Sula's palms as she stood looking at the closed place in the water. They expected him to come back up, laughing. Both girls stared at the water.

Though they both know they are responsible for Chicken Little's drowning, the two girls never tell anyone their terrible secret. At the boy's funeral, Nel stands expressionless while Sula cries uncontrollably. Standing over Chicken Little's grave, they hold hands in a tight clench, then relax slowly, walking home with their fingers laced together in "as gentle a clasp as that of any two young girlfriends trotting up the road on a summer day wondering what happened to butterflies in the winter."

While Nel grows up to be a fairly traditional woman, marrying a man named Jude and settling into the life of a housewife in Medallion, Sula takes off for the larger world, ready for the "experimental life."

"If it wasn't unconventional, she didn't want it," Morrison later said of her conception of Sula's character. "She was willing to risk in her imagination a lot of things and pay the price and also go astray. . . . I wanted to throw her relationship with another woman into relief. Those two women—that too is us, those two desires, to have your adventure *and* safety."

Another thing Morrison wanted to explore in *Sula* was what would happen if one of the friends was to "do the unforgivable thing—to see what that friendship was really made out of."

The "unforgivable thing" that Sula does is to return to Medallion and steal Nel's husband from her. Although she doesn't really love Jude, she seduces him—and then becomes the town pariah, hated by everyone because she seems to have no feelings—no feelings for her old friend Nel, or for Jude, or even for her own mother when she dies in a fire.

But in a strange way, the townspeople also welcome Sula's rebelliousness, her flagrant violations of the social codes of their community.

"Their conviction of Sula's evil," Morrison's narrator tells us, changes "the townspeople in accountable yet mysterious ways." Defining their own lives in contrast to Sula's, they begin to "cherish their husbands and wives, protect their children, repair their homes and in general band together against the devil in their midst."

The bond between Sula and Nel transcends their many years of separation, transcends even Sula's act of betrayal. At the book's end, years after Sula's death, Nel finds herself hearing her old friend's voice in the wind blowing through the treetops down by the old cemetery.

"Sula?" she whispers, "Sula?" and then she realizes that all the years she thought she was missing her husband, she was really missing her old childhood friend.

> And the loss pressed down on her chest and came up in her throat. "We was girls together," she said as though explaining something. "O Lord, Sula," she cried, "girl, girl girlgirlgirl."

Morrison later said that she was interested in portraying Sula and Nel as two halves of one person. "I wanted to say," she told an interviewer from the *Massachusetts Review*, "that there was a little bit of both in each of those two women, and that if they had been one person, I suppose they would have been a rather marvelous person. But each one lacked something that the other had."

Published in December 1973, *Sula* received more critical attention than *The Bluest Eye* had. Selected as an alternate selection by the Book-of-the-Month Club, excerpted in the magazine *Redbook,* and nominated for the 1975 National Book Award in fiction, *Sula* brought Morrison national recognition. There was a slight literary controversy when Sara Blackburn, reviewing the book in the *New York Times Book Review,* suggested that the novel lacked "the stinging immediacy" of Morrison's nonfiction writing and then asserted that "Toni Morrison is far too talented to remain only a marvelous recorder of the black side of provincial American life."

Alice Walker and several other prominent writers wrote letters of protest to the *New York Times,* and Morrison herself had an angry response to Blackburn's criticism: "She's talking about my life. It has a stinging immediacy for *me.*"

Most reviewers, however, were enthusiastic in their praise for *Sula.* The book was hailed by the *Nation* for its originality, and the *Harvard Advocate* noted that Morrison's "characters jump up from the pages vital and strong because she has made us care about the pain in their lives."

Toni Morrison was suddenly much in demand as a public commentator on black life. And it was while giving a lecture on *Sula* that she realized the power her book, with its frank depiction of an unbreakable bond between two women, had to shock and even threaten certain men.

"I went someplace once to talk about *Sula* and there were some genuinely terrified men in the audience," she told the novelist Gloria Naylor, "and they walked out and told me why. They said, 'Friendships between women?' Aghast. Really terrified. You wouldn't think anybody grown-up would display his fear quite that way. But it was such a shocking, threatening thing in a book, let alone what it would be in life."

It would not be the last time Toni Morrison forced her readers to confront things they found shocking or threatening. ❧

5

SONG OF TONI

IN FEBRUARY 1974, Random House published *The Black Book*, an anthology of 300 years of African-American life, which had been compiled by Middleton (Spike) Harris. Edited and largely inspired by Toni Morrison, *The Black Book* is the kind of scrapbook we would have, writes Bill Cosby in the introduction, if "a three-hundred-year-old black man had decided, oh, say, when he was about ten, to keep a record of what it was like for himself and his people in these United States."

In August 1974 Morrison wrote an essay entitled "Rediscovering Black History" for the *New York Times Magazine* in which she explained her excitement about *The Black Book* and her hope that it might enable African Americans to "recognize and rescue those qualities of resistance, excellence, and integrity that were so much a part of our past and so useful to us and to the generations of blacks now growing up."

Morrison with her son Harold. "Sure it's hard, but you do what you have to do," she said to Jean Strouse of Newsweek *in 1981 about the challenges of simultaneously working full-time, raising two children, and writing fiction. "You make time; I don't go to theater or operas or dinners."*

THE

ANTI-SLAVERY RECORD.

VOL. I.   SEPTEMBER, 1835. [SECOND EDITION.]   NO. 9.

THE DESPERATION OF A MOTHER.

" Why do you narrate the extraordinary cases of cruelty ? These stories will not convert the cruel, and they wound the feelings of masters who are not so."
REPLY.   Cruelty is the fruit of the system.

In Marion Co., Missouri, a Negro-Trader was, not long ago, making up a drove for the Red River country.   He purchased two little boys of a planter.   They were to be taken away the next day.   How did the mother of the children feel !   To prevent her interference, she was chained in an out-house.   In the night she contrived to get loose, took an axe, proceeded to the place where her [yes, *her*] boys slept, and severed their heads from their bodies !   She then put an end to her own existence.

☞ The negro-trader and planter quarreled, and went to law, about the *price !*

This illustration and caption appeared in the Anti-Slavery Record, *an abolitionist journal, in 1835 and portray an incident in which a slave mother killed her own two children rather than be forcibly separated from them by sale. The accounts of such tragedies, which Morrison encountered while editing* The Black Book *for Random House, eventually inspired her masterpiece,* Beloved.

As she studied the collected photographs, patents, newspaper clippings, advertisements, recipes, and rent-party jingles that make up *The Black Book*, Morrison was reminded of the stories of black achievement that her parents and grandparents had told her when she was growing up in Lorain.

I felt a renewal of pride I had not felt since 1941, when my parents told me stories of blacks who had invented airplanes, electricity, and shoes. ("Oh, Mama," I cried, "everybody in the world must have had sense enough to wrap his feet." "I am telling you," she replied, "a Negro invented shoes.") And there it was among Spike Harris's collection of patents: the overshoe. The airplane was also there as an airship registered in 1900 by John Pickering. . . .

Working on *The Black Book,* Morrison was also reminded of the brutality so many black Americans had faced under slavery. She sat in Middleton Harris's apartment with a magnifying glass, reading two- and three-hundred-year-old newspaper accounts of the tortures inflicted upon slaves. "Flogging with a leather strap on the naked body is common; also, paddling the body with a hand-saw until the skin is a mass of blisters, and then breaking the blisters with the teeth of the saw."

Amid the rare newspaper clippings she found an 1856 article entitled "A Visit to the Slave Mother Who Killed Her Child," about a runaway slave named Margaret Garner who cut the throat of her own daughter rather than see her returned to the hands of the slaveholders. Years later, this horrific, true-life episode would be the inspiration for *Beloved,* one of Morrison's most acclaimed novels.

In the meantime, the strands of another novel were coming together in Morrison's mind. Her last book, *Sula,* had received so much attention for its portrayal of strong female characters that she became determined to write a novel in which "the men are powerful figures," a story "informed by a male spirit."

Her home life helped contribute to this determination. Raising two sons as a single mother was difficult, even under the best of circumstances, and Morrison was becoming increasingly aware of the many ways in which boys truly are different from girls.

"As boys, my sons were attracted to danger and risk in a way that I was not," Morrison would recall in a radio interview years later. "They had different spatial requirement than girls. And part of that may be education and socialization, but nevertheless, there they were—these male children who tended to eat up the house."

And as she began working on the new book she was tentatively calling *Milkman Dead*, and which would later be published as *Song of Solomon*, she observed her sons' territorial behavior closely.

"I found the boys useful when I was doing *Song of Solomon*," she would later say, "because having watched them grow up, I was able, I think to enter into a male view of the world, which, to me, means a delight in dominion—a definite need to exercise dominion over place and people."

It was a difficult time in Morrison's personal life. There were financial strains in the household. Her oldest son was "entering manhood" ("And if they do that properly, they do it explosively," she would later say. "He was doing it properly.") And, in addition to her hectic schedule of full-time editing and full-time parenting, Morrison had recently added college teaching to her timetable, accepting the position of visiting lecturer at Yale University, a position she would hold for two years. Leaving work at Random House on Friday evenings, she would take the train to New Haven, Connecticut, and teach a course that focused on contemporary black women and their fiction.

Then, to complicate matters even more, Morrison's father died. She returned to Lorain for the funeral, fondly remembering the man who could hold down three jobs at once and, even in the heart of the depression, continue to wear polished Florsheim shoes and natty suits.

"He was the kind of man who was at home anywhere," she later told the *Washington Post*. "Even in joints. He knew the kind of men that didn't belong to my mother's church, but he mellowed and eventually became a church member.

"And I remember one tale. You know how the churches sell dinner—for years—to build a new church. Well, if the church didn't sell all the dinners, my father would take the leftover plates and go sell them in the joints. It was in one of these joints that my father went to sell some barbecue dinners, a joint on Vine Street in Lorain, and these two dudes were getting ready to shoot one another.

"My father walked in and said 'You niggers, put those guns down and you buy this barbecue,'" Morrison recalled. "And so they did. Bought the plates and proceeded to eat the barbecue."

In a way, it was a relief to return to New York after the funeral and get to work on her new novel. Not that she could take her mind off her father's death, though. Thoughts of him stayed very much in Morrison's mind as she began work on the book that would be called *Song of Solomon*; as she sat down to write, she would have long conversations with her father in her head, using his "spirit" to help her develop the characters in the new book.

Writing *Song of Solomon* represented a new kind of challenge for Morrison: in her earlier books, she had written "vignettes of men," but she had never focused an entire novel on their lives, on their "attraction of violence," on "the driving forces behind them."

She centered the novel on a character named Macon Dead III—known to everyone as Milkman—who leaves his home in Michigan and travels to the South in search of the fabled family fortune, a hidden treasure of gold. Although he never finds the gold,

From the American Baptist.

A VISIT TO THE SLAVE MOTHER WHO KILLED HER CHILD.

Last Sabbath, after preaching in the city prison, Cincinnati, through the kindness of the Deputy Sheriff, I was permitted to visit the apartment of that unfortunate woman, concerning whom there has been so much excitement during the last two weeks.

I found her with an infant in her arms only a few months old, and observed that it had a large bunch on its forehead. I inquired the cause of the injury. She then proceeded to give a detailed account of her attempt to kill her children.

She said, that when the officers and slave-hunters came to the house in which they were concealed, she caught a shovel and struck two of her children on the head, and then took a knife and cut the throat of the third, and tried to kill the other,—that if they had given her time, she would have killed them all—that with regard to herself, she cared but little; but she was unwilling to have her children suffer as she had done.

I inquired if she was not excited almost to madness when she committed the act. No, she replied, I was as cool as I now am; and would much rather kill them at once, and thus end their sufferings, than have them taken back to slavery, and be murdered by piece-meal.

She then told the story of her wrongs. She spoke of her days of suffering, of her nights of unmitigated toil, while the bitter tears coursed their way down her cheeks, and fell in the face of the innocent child as it looked smiling up, little conscious of the danger and probable suffering that awaited it.

As I listened to the facts, and witnessed the agony depicted in her countenance, I could not but exclaim, Oh, how terrible is irresponsible power, when exercised over intelligent beings! She alludes to the child that she killed as being free from all trouble and sorrow, with a degree of satisfaction that almost chills the blood in one's veins; yet she evidently possesses all the passionate tenderness of a mother's love. She is about twenty-five years of age, and apparently possesses an average amount of kindness, with a vigorous intellect, and much energy of character.

The two men and the two other children were in another apartment, but her mother-in-law was in the same room. She says she is the mother of eight children, most of whom have been separated from her; that her husband was once separated from her twenty-five years, during which time she did not see him; that could she have prevented it, she would never have permitted him to return, as she did not wish him to witness her sufferings, or be exposed to the brutal treatment that he would receive.

She states that she has been a faithful servant, and in her old age she would not have attempted to obtain her liberty; but as she became feeble, and less capable of performing labor, her master became more and more exacting and brutal in his treatment, until she could stand it no longer; that the effort could result only in death, at most—she therefore made the attempt.

She witnessed the killing of the child, but said she neither encouraged nor discouraged her daughter-in-law,—for under similar circumstances she should probably have done the same. The old woman is from sixty to seventy years of age, has been a professor of religion about twenty years, and speaks with much feeling of the time when she shall be delivered from the power of the oppressor, and dwell with the Savior, 'where the wicked cease from troubling, and the weary are at rest.'

These slaves (as far as I am informed) have resided all their lives within sixteen miles of Cincinnati. We are frequently told that Kentucky slavery is very innocent. If these are its fruits, where it exists in a mild form, will some one tell us what we may expect from its more objectionable features? But comments are unnecessary.   P. S. BASSETT.

Fairmount Theological Seminary,
Cincinnati, (Ohio,) Feb. 12, 1856.

This 1856 article by P. S. Bassett, a Baptist minister in Cincinnati, Ohio, describes his visit to an imprisoned runaway slave who tried to kill her children rather than have them returned to slavery and was the specific inspiration for Beloved.

Milkman finds something much more important along the way—an understanding of the spiritual treasure which is his rich family history.

As he journeys through the South, one of Milkman's most important clues to his background comes from the "Song of Solomon," a nursery rhyme he overhears some children singing as they play a game in a little Virginia town. The song is remarkably like the one Milkman's mystical aunt Pilate had sung when he was a boy:

> Sugarman done fly away
> Sugarman done gone
> Sugarman cut across the sky
> Sugarman gone home.

But these children in Virginia do not sing a song about "Sugarman," they use the name "Solomon." Milkman suddenly realizes that the song is part of his own family history, and that the "Solomon" the children are singing about is his great-grandfather, a slave who, according to the legend, was able to escape his bondage by flying back to Africa.

Song of Solomon is a sweeping epic of a novel, and Morrison relates much more than the story of Milkman's quest for his family heritage. She also gives us perhaps one of her greatest characters in the fiery Pilate, a strange and magical woman, born without a navel, whose name—like that of Morrison's own mother, Ramah—was chosen at random from the pages of the Bible.

And there is a remarkable subplot involving Milkman's friend Guitar, who joins a secret society called the Seven Days, a vigilante group that kills white people at random in revenge for the murder of blacks.

The novel ends with Milkman, having discovered the secrets of his family history, leaping fearlessly from a cliff, convinced that he now knows what his ancestors knew: that "if you surrendered to the air, you could *ride* it."

Morrison drew on many aspects of her own family background in writing *Song of Solomon*. The children's song that Milkman hears was actually a song that came from the branch of Morrison's family in Alabama. They sang a version that went, "Green, the only son of Solomon."

And the myth of the flying Africans was something Morrison had heard about throughout her childhood. Many slave narratives talk of blacks who could fly, and there is a famous African-American folktale about a group of African-born slaves who rise up from the plantation and fly back home across the ocean. Asked about this legend after *Song of Solomon* was published, Morrison told an interviewer that, although there are parallels to the famous Greek myth about Icarus, the meaning she intended in her novel was very specific to the African-American experience.

"It is about black people who could fly," she told the *New Republic.* "That was always part of the folklore of my life; flying was one of our gifts. I don't care how silly it may seem. It was everywhere— people used to talk about it, it's in the spirituals and gospels. Perhaps it was wishful thinking—escape, death, and all that. But suppose it wasn't. What might it mean? I tried to find out in *Song of Solomon*."

The publication of *Song of Solomon* in 1977 would change Toni Morrison's life in a fundamental way. No longer an aspiring writer, she was hailed by critics as a literary giant, her interweaving of realism with the supernatural compared to the work of the Nobel Prize–winning Colombian novelist Gábriel García Márquez.

For the first time since she began writing, she felt confident enough to call herself "a writer." Before that she had always told people that she was "a teacher who writes," or "an editor who writes"—but now, being a novelist was undoubtedly, if not her only, then certainly her foremost occupation.

Song of Solomon was something of a national sensation, the first novel by a black writer to become a Book-of-the-Month Club selection since Richard Wright's *Native Son* back in 1940. Morrison received the National Book Critics Circle Award in 1977 and an appointment to the American Academy and Institute of Arts and Letters. A year later, when *Song of Solomon* was a paperback best-seller with 570,000 copies in print, President Jimmy Carter appointed her to the prestigious National Council on the Arts.

But Morrison was not one to rest on her laurels. She kept up her rigorous daily routine, working at Random House, lecturing at Yale on Fridays, and, of course, doing her best to play both "father and mother" for her two sons.

It was while driving her oldest son to his piano lesson in Manhattan, shortly after *Song of Solomon* had been published, that Morrison first fully realized the scope of her sudden fame.

Dropping Harold at his music teacher's, Morrison had an hour to kill, so she drove her car around and passed by a Doubleday bookstore in midtown Manhattan that had a large display of books in the window. Suddenly, she recognized the cover of *Song of Solomon*. She drove around to the other side of the store, stopped the car, and saw a lovely array of her books. There was also a huge sign in the window that read "A Triumph, by Toni Morrison."

She sat silently in the car. It took her a few moments to believe it was really her they were talking about. ❦

March 30, 1981 / $1.25

Newsweek

Black Magic

Novelist
Toni
Morrison

6

LICKETY-SPLIT, LICKETY-SPLIT

T HERE WAS A certain story that always terrified Toni Morrison as a child, though she was never quite sure why. It was the story of the tar baby, a traditional African-American folktale dating back to the days of slavery, and it would become the inspiration for Morrison's next novel.

The tar baby legend comes from a tradition of oral storytelling known as trickster tales. Although it was popularized by the white American writer Joel Chandler Harris in his Uncle Remus plantation stories of the 1880s, it is actually part of a very old folkloric tradition with origins in West Africa. Variations of legends involving trickster characters such as Br'er Rabbit were common throughout black communities in both America and the Caribbean.

In the version of the tar baby story Morrison heard as a child, a white farmer makes a concoction of tar and turpentine, dresses it in a bonnet and skirt, and sets it out to trap the troublesome rabbit that has been raiding his garden. Br'er Rabbit approaches the tar baby and says "good morning," but when the tar baby doesn't respond, Br'er Rabbit punches it, and just as the farmer had planned, gets his paw stuck in the tar.

The farmer arrives and the clever Br'er Rabbit begs, "Boil me in oil, skin me alive, but please don't throw me in that briar patch!"

Newsweek took the occasion of the publication of Tar Baby, Morrison's fourth novel, to put the author on the cover of its March 30, 1981, issue.

The farmer falls for the trick and throws him straight into the briar patch. As Br'er Rabbit runs away—lickety-split, lickety-split—he taunts the farmer, singing, "This is where I was born and bred at!"

By the time Morrison heard the story, as a small girl, the word "tar baby" had also become a racial slur, a name used particularly for black girls. And as she began to think more about the legend, it seemed odd to her that tar would play such an important role in an American story. Beginning her research, she soon discovered a character known as a "tar lady" in African mythology.

"I started thinking about tar," she told an interviewer. "At one time, a tar pit was a holy place, at least an important place, because tar was used to build things. It came naturally out of the earth; it held together things like Moses's little boat and the pyramids. For me, the tar baby came to mean the black woman who can hold things together."

Setting out to write her fourth novel, Morrison would use the tar baby legend to construct a modern-day allegory. *Tar Baby*, published in 1981, was Morrison's first novel to depict fully developed white characters interacting with blacks. It was also her first novel not set in the black communities of the American Midwest and South.

As she had in *Song of Solomon*, Morrison steeped her new novel in black folklore. The action of *Tar Baby* takes place primarily on a small fictitious island in the Caribbean, Isle des Chevaliers, named after a group of mythical African horsemen. According to the legend Morrison gives us in *Tar Baby*, these Africans were brought to the island as slaves, but escaped their captivity and are said to be roaming the hills of Isle des Chevaliers on horseback.

Against this mythical backdrop, Morrison employs a modern love story to update the folktale of the tar baby and Br'er Rabbit. In Morrison's novel the character of Jadine, a beautiful, jet-setting black model, parallels that of the tar baby. Jadine is the niece of Sydney and Ondine Childs, the butler and cook to a retired white millionaire named Valerian Street who lives in an estate on Isle des Chevaliers. Valerian Street has paid for Jadine's education in Paris, and in his home she is treated like an elegant house guest.

When a dreadlocked outlaw named Son arrives on the island uninvited, his presence in the Street mansion brings out all of the family's ugliest secrets. Jadine and Son eventually fall in love and run away to America, but in the end neither one can adapt to the other's way of life. Cut off from the "ancient properties" of her ancestors, Jadine cannot live with Son in his "briar patch," nor can Son adapt to the superficial glamour of her New York life. In one of the book's climactic scenes, Son angrily rapes Jadine and tells her the story of the tar baby, implying that just like the tar baby, she is something "made" by a white man.

And though he seems to despise Jadine and all her materialistic values, Son is also obsessed with her. By the end of the novel he is desperately trying to break free from the emotional hold of this fiery woman, but wondering how he will ever be able to let go of a woman "whose face was enough to engage your attention all your life . . . a woman who was not only a woman but a sound, all the music he had ever wanted to play, a world and a way of being in it. . . ." How, Son wonders, returning to Isle des Chevaliers, will he be able to "let that go?"

By the time *Tar Baby* was published in March of 1981, Toni Morrison was beginning at last to live the life of a successful author. The best-selling *Song of Solomon* had made her, if not wealthy, then certainly financially secure. She and her sons had moved from

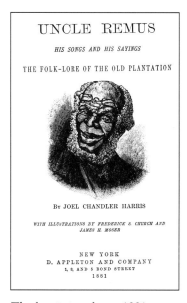

The frontispiece for an 1881 edition of Joel Chandler Harris's Uncle Remus, His Songs and Sayings. *Uncle Remus was a fictional character created by Harris, a white journalist, as the narrator of the various black folk tales from the days of slavery that he had collected. In her fourth novel, Morrison used the tar baby tale related by Harris as a metaphor for the resiliency of black Americans.*

Morrison credits her experience raising her two sons, Harold (left) and Slade, for her ability to accurately depict male characters. "I learned a lot from my sons, seeing how excited they got by going near danger, for instance— they'd come away charged, lifted, as if somebody'd turned the volume up," she told Jean Strouse.

Queens to a four-story converted boat house in Rockland County, less than an hour's drive from New York City. The house was located right on the Hudson River, with its own private dock, and had an old-fashioned porch with a swinging bench on which Morrison could sit during the summertime and write.

The first time Morrison saw the house, she took a long walk along the dock, stared at the view of the river for many minutes, and could almost hear her father's voice telling her how much he approved.

After *Song of Solomon*, Morrison decided to cut back on her editing duties at Random House, working only about one full day a week in New York and devoting much more of her time to fiction writing, which she preferred to do in the early morning hours. She enjoyed getting up before 5:00 A.M. so that she could watch the sun rise as she worked. She continued her college teaching schedule; though no longer at Yale, she now both lectured at Bard College in upstate New York and was appointed an associate professor at the State University of New York at Purchase.

By the late 1970s Toni Morrison had become something of a national celebrity, profiled in the *New*

York Times Magazine and the subject of numerous radio and television interviews. But now, with the publication of *Tar Baby*, Morrison was to receive an unprecedented degree of media attention.

"Are you really going to put a middle-aged, gray-haired colored lady on the cover of this magazine?" she asked, laughingly, on a visit to the offices of *Newsweek*, early in 1981.

She did indeed appear on the cover of the March 30, 1981, issue of *Newsweek*, the first black woman in the magazine's history to be so honored. Articles about Morrison would follow shortly in most of the country's other leading magazines and newspapers.

Almost every interviewer and reporter who spoke to Morrison seemed to be astonished by the sheer range of her activities: raising two sons on her own, working full-time as a senior editor, teaching college—all in addition to writing four novels that had now secured her place among the pantheon of America's most influential authors.

But Morrison resisted any effort to portray her as some kind of "superwoman." Fixing breakfast for her son Harold while being interviewed by *Newsweek*, she was asked how she could possibly find time amid her busy schedule to write.

"Sure it's hard," she said, "but you do what you have to do. You make time; I don't go to theater or operas or dinners. But I think women dwell quite a bit on the duress under which they work, on how hard it is just to do it at all. We are traditionally rather proud of ourselves for having slipped creative work in there between the domestic chores and obligations. I'm not sure we deserve such big A-pluses for all that."

From her father, who had held down three jobs at once during the height of the Great Depression, Morrison had early on learned the secret of making the most of your time.

The *Newsweek* cover story also stressed the enormous impact Morrison was having on her fellow writers and artists.

"She paints pictures with words," observed the opera singer Leontyne Price, "and reading or hearing those words is like listening to music."

"That voice of hers is so sure," said the writer Toni Cade Bambara, whose own literary career Morrison had helped develop as an editor at Random House. "She lures you in, locks the doors and encloses you in a special, very particular universe—all in the first three pages."

"I have a sense of Toni as a mythic character—as somehow larger than life," the novelist Mary Gordon told *Newsweek.* "I once dreamed that she bought a huge old Victorian mansion. It would one day be beautiful, but now it was a wreck, with cobwebs, broken windows, mice, rats and vermin everywhere. I asked her how she was going to deal with all that mess. She simply said, 'No problem,' and waved her arms in the air. Immediately the rats and roaches disappeared and the house was beautiful."

Like *Song of Solomon* before it, *Tar Baby* was a solid commercial success, remaining on the best-seller lists for four months. The critical response to the new book, however, was somewhat mixed. While there was no denying Morrison's masterful use of language and folklore, some critics objected to her "convoluted" plot structure and "stereotypical" characters. Many reviewers felt that Morrison was not at her best working in settings dominated by white culture. Nonetheless, most critics agreed that, whatever the book's flaws, they were due largely to the enormous ambition of Morrison's artistic vision.

"One of fiction's pleasures is to have your mind scratched and your intellectual habits challenged," wrote Webster Schott in the *Washington Post Book World.* "While *Tar Baby* has shortcomings, lack of provocation isn't one of them. Morrison owns a powerful intelligence. It's run by courage. She calls to account conventional wisdom and accepted attitude at nearly every turn."

As the 1980s began, Toni Morrison was becoming more outspoken on social issues, decrying the Reagan administration's budgetary cutbacks on artistic programs at a meeting of the National Council on the Arts. And she was also asserting her role as one of the country's most articulate spokesmen on African-American cultural affairs, vocally criticizing the double standard so often applied—even by well-meaning whites—to black writers. Readers who willingly struggle through the cultural complexities of a work of literature set in Victorian or medieval England, she argued, act strangely put-upon when asked to enter into the unfamiliar territory of a novel that takes place in an African-American milieu.

"People do say, 'I know you're writing black novels, but I was really interested,'" she told an interviewer from *Vogue* magazine, noting that, while such condescending attitudes used to offend her deeply, she had mastered the art of the appropriately sarcastic response. Told once by a white reader how difficult it was to understand the black culture and language in her books, she quipped, "Boy, you must have had a hell of a time with *Beowulf*."

She had learned long ago that humor generally makes for the most effective weapon when confronting the patronizing attitudes that often accompany racist thinking. After taping an episode of the Dick Cavett talk show in New York, Cavett turned to his guest and asked if it wouldn't have been nice to do the whole hour without mentioning the word "black."

"I guess so," Morrison told him with a wry smile, "but you started it." ❧

7

DREAMING BELOVED

◖◗

TONI MORRISON LEFT her position as an editor at Random House in 1983 after 20 years. Her editorial career had been a long and productive one—she had presided over some of the landmark moments of the African-American literary awakening of the 1970s, such as the publication of *The Black Book* and Ivan Van Sertima's *They Came Before Columbus;* and she had helped develop the careers of other notable black women writers such as Gayl Jones and Toni Cade Bambara.

But while her career as an editor was coming to a close, Morrison's involvement in the academic world was just beginning to blossom. In 1984, she was named the Albert Schweitzer Professor of the Humanities at the State University of New York in Albany. In her new position as professor of creative writing and African-American literature, she would conduct small fiction seminars with several young writers on fellowships at the university. Her role was to help them "to put their writing in the middle of their lives," as she later described it.

"She's brilliant and inspiring," F. R. Lewis, one of her graduate students, told the *New York Times.* "She's not trying to sell you a writing style or method. She's not trying to turn out little Toni Morrisons. She's looking for individual voices and personal visions underpinning our work. She has tremendous authority and

"Writing and reading are not all that distinct for a writer," Morrison wrote in 1993. *"Both exercises require being alert and ready for unaccountable beauty ... for the world that imagination evokes."*

The tragic story of Emmett Till (pictured here) was the basis for Morrison's play Dreaming Emmett. *Though one of the accused murderers later confessed to the crime in a national magazine, the all-white jury acquitted the trio after a brief deliberation.*

presence, but she still sits, takes her shoes off and puts her feet up on the table. She's a person."

It was while in Albany that Morrison began work on her first play, *Dreaming Emmett*. The idea for the play had actually come to her several years earlier, but she didn't begin to write it until arriving in Albany and meeting William Kennedy, the Pulitzer prize–winning novelist and director of the New York State Writers Institute. The Writers Institute commissioned Morrison to write a dramatic work in commemoration of the first federal holiday celebrating the birthday of Dr. Martin Luther King, Jr.

Strictly speaking, *Dreaming Emmett* was not Morrison's first foray into the theater. Several years earlier, she had written the book and the lyrics for a musical called *New Orleans*, which was staged at the Public Theater in New York. But Morrison never considered the musical one of her own artistic works, because the idea for *New Orleans* wasn't hers; the play was written more or less "like an assignment."

With *Dreaming Emmett*, Morrison turned her attention to the true story of Emmett Till, a black Chicago teenager who, while visiting his uncle in Mississippi in 1955, was accused of whistling at a white woman in a store. Till was abducted by racist whites, shot in the head, tied to a cotton-gin fan, and thrown into a river. The Emmett Till murder became something of a cause célèbre for the civil rights movement; the fact that the white men who were charged with his murder were later acquitted by an all-white jury emphasized the inability of African Americans to obtain justice in the Jim Crow South.

Reflecting on the Till murder, Morrison found herself thinking about the "ease with which black children are killed by other people. I was wondering about the conditions going on in 1955 and what's going on in 1985," she told a reporter prior to the play's premiere on January 4, 1986, at the Marketplace Theater in Albany.

In Morrison's version of the Emmett Till story, the 14-year-old is able to come back and tell in his own words the story of his brutal murder. "This is a play about a boy's imagination," Morrison said. "If you unleash the imagination and intelligence of a young black kid, what would he do? What is it like if his dreams are fulfilled?"

Morrison's next literary project would also have its origins in a shockingly violent historical incident—this one dating back to the days of slavery.

In 1851, a slave named Margaret Garner escaped from her master in Kentucky and fled with her four children to the North, to a small neighborhood outside Cincinnati, Ohio, where she sought refuge with her mother-in-law, who was already free. When she was tracked down by her master's slave-catchers, Margaret Garner attempted to kill three of her children so that they would not be returned to the horrific life of slavery. She grabbed a shovel and smashed two of her children in the head, and then took a knife and cut the throat of another. Although only one of the children died, Garner later said that she would gladly have seen all four of her children dead and "thus end their suffering," rather "than have them taken back to slavery, and thus murdered by piecemeal."

Morrison had learned of the Margaret Garner story more than a decade earlier while compiling the materials for *The Black Book* with Middleton Harris. It was in Harris's apartment that she pored over an 1856 article entitled "A Visit to the Slave Mother Who Killed Her Child," which appeared in a publication called the *American Baptist*. What struck Morrison most about the story was that even after she was imprisoned for the murder of her own child, Garner remained completely calm and secure in her resolve that she had done the right thing. There was no changing her conviction. She showed no remorse: she was simply "unwilling to have her children suffer as she had done." For Toni Morrison, this was an introduction to "a despair quite new to me but so deep it had no passion at all and elicited no tears."

For many years after learning of the Garner incident, Morrison wanted to write her tale, but found that she was unable to do so. She felt at first that the story could not be written, but then became "annoyed and worried that such a story was inaccessible to art. If I couldn't do it, I felt really sold. In the end, I had to rely on the resilience and power of the characters—if they could live it all of their lives, I could write it."

As she began work on the novel that would be published as *Beloved*, Morrison made a conscious decision not to learn too much about the real-life Margaret Garner. To enter into the mind of the slave woman who would be the protagonist of her book, she needed to employ her full imaginative powers and not be bound to the literal facts of the Garner story. She did not want to "document" the life of Margaret Garner, but rather use the tragic episode of child-murder as a starting point and invent another life for her.

Soon, the character who began to take shape in Morrison's mind was no longer called Margaret Garner but Sethe. "I listen to the characters and ask what their names are," Morrison told an interviewer. "It's a process that is very respectful." Like Garner, Sethe would be a runaway slave from Kentucky; and, as in the true-life story, she would take the life of her daughter rather than see the child returned to the hands of the slave owners.

But Morrison set the story of *Beloved* in the years following the Civil War, when Sethe is struggling to create a new life for herself in Ohio. She lives with her surviving daughter, Denver, and her mother-in-law, Baby Suggs, in a farmhouse on the outskirts of Cincinnati. The house on 124 Bluestone Road, called simply "124," is haunted by the ghost of the baby whose throat Sethe cut with a handsaw some eighteen years before. One hundred twenty-four is a "spiteful" house, "full of a baby's venom": mirrors break, furniture flies, and baby handprints appear as if by magic in cake icing.

With the arrival of Paul D., the "last of the Sweet Home men"—as the male slaves on Sethe's former Kentucky plantation were known—the domestic situation in 124 is thrown into further turmoil. Paul D. violently tries to cast out the baby's spirit and appears to have succeeded until one day a beautiful 20-year-old stranger with a scar on her throat arrives at 124. She cannot explain where she has come from, and she calls herself simply Beloved. (Years earlier, when burying her murdered child, Sethe did not have enough money to engrave the words "Dearly Beloved" on the tombstone, and had settled for just "Beloved.")

Beloved takes control of the household and nearly destroys Sethe, until a group of former slave women, who have long ostracized Sethe because of the murder, join together to help exorcise the ghost of Beloved at last.

While much of the action of *Beloved* takes place in the years after the Civil War, Morrison also gives us many powerful flashbacks of life during slavery, depicting the atrocities inflicted on Paul D. and on Sethe by men like the sadistic slave owner known as "the schoolteacher" who regarded their slaves as subhuman property.

Morrison did extensive research into this period, even traveling to Brazil to study the horrific implements employed by slave-masters. She was particularly interested in learning about a notorious implement of torture called "the bit," but she could not find

Blacks at work on a Mississippi plantation. In preparation for the writing of Beloved, *Morrison studied the history and literature of slavery.*

much information on it in the United States. Many American slave museums, she found, "try to be upbeat," displaying "quilts and all the 'cute' things slaves did." During her travels to Brazil, though, she found implements of torture like the bit—a cage the slave was put in that had metal tongues that could be tightened in the back—and the masks slaves were forced to wear while cutting sugar cane. "They had holes in them, but it was so hot inside that when they took them off, the skin would come off.

"What is interesting is that these things were not restraining tools, like in the torture chamber. They were things you wore while you were doing the work." It seemed to Morrison "that the humiliation was the key to what the experience was like."

Morrison dedicated *Beloved* to the "Sixty million and more" who perished under slavery. "I asked some scholars to estimate for me the number of black people who died in 200 years of slavery," she explained. "Those 60 million are people who didn't make it from there to here and through. Some people told me 40 million, but I also heard 60 million, and I didn't want to leave anybody out."

She read accounts of slavers traveling on the Congo River who reported that they could not get their boats through the water owing to the logjam of bodies. And the survival rate for the Middle Passage—during which slaves were transported in atrocious conditions from Africa to the Americas—was abysmally low.

"Slave trade was like cocaine is now," Morrison said in a *Time* magazine interview. "Even though it was against the law, that didn't stop anybody. Imagine getting $1,000 for a human being. That's a lot of money. There are fortunes in this country that were made that way."

But Morrison stressed that her novel was not about the institution of slavery "with a capital S,"

An 18th-century illustration of slaves shackled in the hold of their ship for the Middle Passage from Africa to the Americas. Morrison dedicated Beloved *to the 60 million blacks who had died as the result of slavery.*

but about "these anonymous people called slaves. What they do to keep on, how they make a life, what they're willing to risk, however long it lasts, in order to relate to one another."

Published in 1987, *Beloved* was an immediate best-seller and was quickly acclaimed as Morrison's most powerful book to date. The novelist Margaret Atwood, writing in the *New York Times Book Review*, called the book "a triumph," adding that Morrison's "versatility and technical and emotional range appear to know no bounds." John Leonard, writing in the *Los Angeles Times*, called *Beloved* "a masterwork," belonging "on the highest shelf of American literature.... Without *Beloved* our imagination of the nation's self has a hole in it big enough to die from." And *London Times* reviewer Nicholas Shakespeare likened the book to the "first singing of a people hardened by their suffering, people who have been hanged and whipped and mortgaged at the hands of [white people]. . . . From Toni Morrison's pen it is a sound that breaks the back of words, making *Beloved* a great novel."

But the triumphant publication of *Beloved* was marred by a moment of minor controversy in Morrison's career. Despite being widely hailed as Morrison's masterpiece, the book failed to win either the annual National Book Award or the National Book Critics Circle Award in 1987. In January 1988, 48 prominent black writers and critics—outraged over the lack of recognition Morrison's novel had thus far received—signed a tribute to her achievements that was published in the *New York Times Book Review*. The letter noted that the author James Baldwin had recently died without ever having been recognized with either the National Book Award or the Pulitzer Prize and remarked on the "oversight and harmful whimsy" that had so far denied either prestigious award to Morrison.

Morrison herself said later that she was unaware of the statement before its publication in the *New York Times Book Review*. Certain critics viewed the letter as a thinly veiled attempt to intimidate the Pulitzer Prize committee, while others felt that, should *Beloved* be awarded the Pulitzer Prize for fiction, the novel's undeniable brilliance would now be tainted by the controversy surrounding the signed "manifesto."

The matter was settled on March 31, 1988, when *Beloved* was indeed awarded the Pulitzer Prize for fiction. Most literary figures agreed that the novel had won based on its own obvious merits. Novelist Ralph Ellison, whose classic *Invisible Man* received the National Book Award in 1953, was one of the few leading black writers who had refused to sign the letter to the *New York Times Book Review*.

"Good for Toni," Ellison said, upon learning of the Pulitzer committee's decision. "I was pretty annoyed with some of the stuff that's been boiling. Toni doesn't need that kind of support, even though it can be well-intentioned. She can compete with the best writers anywhere."

Morrison herself expressed gratitude for the sentiment—if not the timing—of her colleagues' statement.

"That was kind of a blessing for me," Morrison told the *New York Times*, "to know that irrespective of the formal recognition that is available to a writer,

Ralph Ellison, the author of Invisible Man, *one of the most influential novels of African-American life ever written, was a consistent champion of Morrison's work, although he did not join with other writers in protesting her failure to win the National Book Award in 1987.*

that they appreciated the worth of my work to them. They redeemed me, but I am certain they played no significant role in the judgment."

Now 57, with five novels to her name, the woman who was born Chloe Anthony Wofford had at last been recognized with one of America's highest literary honors, an achievement that must have seemed unimaginable to the little schoolgirl poring over her copy of *Madame Bovary* at her desk so many years ago in Lorain, Ohio.

"I am glad that the merits of the book were allowed to surface and be the only consideration of the Pulitzer Prize committee," Morrison said in a formal statement issued from her office in Albany. "I hope the Pulitzer board is as proud of me as I am of them. It is a singular honor and I am deeply pleased."

There was in fact still quite a lot of the playful little girl in this award-winning author. While working on *Beloved*, Morrison later said, she had begun to believe in her supernatural central character, in the ghost of the dead girl that comes back to haunt her mother. She would often find herself looking at a chair in the corner of the room and wondering if it had moved a little bit on its own.

And she would sit for hours, lost in her fantasy world, imagining she was Sethe and dreaming of her lost baby, picturing Beloved entering the kitchen and pouring herself a cup of coffee.

"You have to suspend disbelief long enough, because if I don't believe it, you can't make anybody else believe it," she told an interviewer from the Associated Press. "You have to give [your readers] a shot, by saying, 'Yeah, I happen to know that you're really afraid of ghosts and the reason I know this is because you were a kid once, weren't you? And you didn't really believe that was a branch at the windows, and didn't you sleep with your hands behind the bed because you knew something was underneath?'"

"I have to go back to that place myself," Morrison explained. "If I left the closet door open in the bedroom when I was a kid, anything might come out, and my mother would have to come and shut the door. All of that, it's child stuff, but that's us. Those things are not just there because we're short." ✿

8

JAZZ AGE

This photograph was used to promote the publication of Morrison's sixth novel, Jazz, *which had initially been conceived as the second of three parts (*Beloved *was the first) of a sprawling single novel.*

ONI MORRISON WAS named the Robert F. Goheen Professor in the Council of Humanities at Princeton University on November 8, 1987. Leaving behind her position at the State University of New York in Albany and arriving on the pristine New Jersey campus in the spring of 1989, she became the first African-American woman writer to hold a named chair at an Ivy League university.

"I take teaching as seriously as I do my writing," Morrison said of her decision to accept the professorship. "Princeton's notion of what constitutes serious teaching dovetails with mine. You can get a small number of students who are working on projects and stay with them for a year or even two."

In the late 1980s, Princeton was in the process of building one of the country's leading African-American studies programs, attracting not only Morrison but leading black scholars like Cornell West and Arnold Rampersand. This was quite a turnaround for an elite university whose doors, for many years, had been completely closed to blacks, Jews, and women. The great African-American singer, actor, and political activist Paul Robeson had actually grown up in the town of Princeton, where his father was a prominent clergyman; but despite being one of the nation's outstanding scholar-athletes, Robeson could not attend the university because of his color,

This photograph from James Van Der Zee's The Harlem Book of the Dead *was Morrison's initial inspiration for* Jazz.

and went instead to nearby Rutgers, where he enjoyed an outstanding academic and athletic career.

Toni Morrison's duties at Princeton would be interdisciplinary—she would teach in the creative writing program and also participate in the African-American studies, American studies, and women's studies departments. Of course, even as she immersed herself in the demanding life of Ivy League academia, she was already hard at work on a new novel. The tragic events of the Margaret Garner story that she had retold and refashioned in *Beloved* had actually been conceived as just one part of a much larger novel, a novel with three independent sections and three time frames. While the first story was set in post–Civil War Ohio, the second narrative would jump forward to the 1920s and to the community that was then the undisputed center for black life in America: Harlem, New York.

It was Morrison's editor at Alfred A. Knopf, who realized that the sprawling story Morrison had envisioned should be broken up into separate novels. Well past her deadline, Morrison brought the unfinished 275-page manuscript to her editor, saying, "I'm very sorry that I'm two years late, but I'm not going to be able to finish." The editor read the section about Sethe, Beloved, and the supernatural goings-on at 124 Bluestone Road and immediately saw it not only as a self-contained novel but as a literary masterpiece.

And just as *Beloved* had grown out of an obscure 19th-century news clipping, Morrison's next novel was inspired by a photograph she had seen many years before in a book called *The Harlem Book of the Dead*, a collection of pictures of deceased black New Yorkers taken in the 1920s by the photographer James Van Der Zee. It was the macabre fashion of the time to have photographs of deceased loved ones taken, dressed up in their finest clothes, lying elegantly in their coffins. Sometimes parents would even have photographs taken of themselves cradling a dead child in their arms.

The story behind one of the photographs in *The Harlem Book of the Dead* was especially intriguing to Morrison: it was a picture of a dead girl lying in a coffin, and the text explained that she was just 18 years old and had been dancing at a "rent party" when she suddenly slumped over. Her friends rushed to her side and, seeing the blood streaming out of her, realized that she must have been shot by someone.

"What happened to you?" her friends asked.

"I'll tell you tomorrow," the dying girl said. "I'll tell you tomorrow."

She knew all along that her jealous ex-boyfriend had been the one who shot her, using a silencer on his gun, but the girl still loved him enough to want him to get away safely.

For Morrison, the girl's actions represented the epitome of "romantic, teenage passion," of loving someone so much that you feel you can't live without them. This tale of doomed love had parallels to the story of Margaret Garner, who'd loved her daughter so much she had taken her life rather than return her to a life of slavery. And, just as in the Margaret Garner story, the anecdote surrounding this murdered Harlem girl was the story of a woman who had "placed all of the value of her life in something outside herself."

Morrison constructed her novel as a romantic triangle, the story of Joe Trace, a middle-aged door-to-door cosmetics salesman; his wife, Violet, a beautician; and Joe's lover, Dorcas, a teenager whose parents had been murdered in the notorious East St. Louis race riots of 1919.

In a technique she had developed in her first novel, *The Bluest Eye*, Morrison lays out the entire drama of *Jazz* in the very first paragraph of the very first page:

> Sth, I know that woman. She used to live with a flock of birds on Lenox Avenue. Know her husband, too. He fell for an eighteen-year-old girl with one of those deepdown, spooky loves that made him so sad and happy he shot her just to keep the feeling going.

"That woman," Joe's wife Violet, becomes so obsessed with her husband's young lover that she even crashes the funeral and tries to disfigure Dorcas's face with a butcher knife.

Alongside this tale of anguished love, *Jazz* is also a rhapsody to New York City, which Morrison's narrator refers to throughout the book simply as "the City." *Jazz* depicts that exciting period in American history when Southern blacks—like Joe and Violet Trace—were migrating in great numbers to northern cities, transplanting what had been a traditionally rural culture to an urban environment. It was a time of exceptional vitality in African-American cultural life. African-American music and dance became so emblematic of the national mood that, even for white authors like F. Scott Fitzgerald, the glittering, high-flying 1920s were best summed up by the phrase "the Jazz Age."

Harlem was the intellectual and artistic hub for this awakening in black American life, home to a vibrant community of writers and artists like Langston Hughes and Countee Cullen as well as to visionary black American political leaders like the Pan-Africanist Marcus Garvey. Perhaps more than anything else, though, Harlem became known as a vibrant center for music and dance. "You can take the A-Train," went the lyric to a classic Duke Ellington tune, and throughout the 1920s white New Yorkers, from mobsters to socialites, flocked to nightspots like the Cotton Club on 125th Street to hear the great jazz artists of the day such as Ellington, Cab Calloway, and Bessie Smith.

But although Morrison is clearly writing about the Jazz Age in the novel, she is not interested in depicting the celebrities of the period. In fact, other than the title, the word "jazz" appears nowhere in the book. Morrison's characters are the average working people of Harlem, people who are not even aware that they are living through a period that would, in later years, be known as the Harlem Renaissance or the Jazz Age.

"I wanted the book to really be about the people who didn't know they were living in an 'era,'" Morrison told a TV interviewer after the book's publication. "The same thing is true for Sethe in *Beloved*—she didn't know she was a classic example of something. . . . These were ordinary people. Jazz was for ordinary people; jazz *is* ordinary people."

With her sixth novel slated for publication in 1992, Toni Morrison was also compiling a series of lectures she had delivered at Harvard University for publication as the critical study *Playing in the Dark: Whiteness and the Literary Imagination.*

The book is a broad critique of some of the classic writers of American literature, from Edgar Allan Poe and Mark Twain through Ernest Hemingway and Willa Cather, in which Morrison argues that the language and culture of black Americans have played a more significant role in the development of American literature than most white writers are willing to acknowledge.

Citing examples from works such as Twain's *Huckleberry Finn* and Hemingway's *To Have and Have Not*, Morrison argues that, throughout American literature, white authors have frequently repressed or negated their black characters; and she calls upon her fellow critics and scholars to take up the study of what she terms "American Africanism" in literature.

Both *Jazz* and *Playing in the Dark* were published early in 1992, and despite their obvious dissimilarities, the two books were jointly reviewed in many newspapers and magazines. In contrast to the almost unanimous critical acclaim accorded *Beloved*, the response to *Jazz* was more muted. Edna O'Brien, the Irish novelist, reviewed the novel in the *New York Times Book Review*, praising Morrison's "virtuosity" and her ability to "conjur[e] up worlds with complete authority," but ultimately faulting the book for its lack of an "emotional nexus." Richard Eder, on the

Morrison (middle) with the great jazz vocalist Ella Fitzgerald. Jazz was the music of Harlem in the 1920s, which is the setting of Morrison's sixth novel.

other hand, writing in the *Los Angeles Times Book Review*, called the book "a half-waking dream on a lumpy corncob mattress" and argued that *Jazz* was an even finer novel than *Beloved*. And John Leonard, in a lengthy rumination on Morrison's career in the *Nation*, singled out *Jazz* for its "radiance and genius" and concluded that, "with her wit, poetry and passion, breadth of sympathy, depth of feeling, range of interest, grasp of detail, powers of imaginative transformation, command of time, character, scruple, generosity and radiance, and magical mastery of the Mother Tongue," Morrison is "the best writer working in America."

The critical response to *Playing in the Dark* was somewhat less enthusiastic. Morrison's analysis of the "Africanist presence" in American literature came at a time when American literary circles were already highly polarized in the debate on such issues as "multiculturalism" and the proposed revisions to the established "canon" of literary masterworks. While *Playing in the Dark* received polite notices in a number of publications, Morrison's first critical collection was harshly reviewed in neoconservative magazines such as the *New Republic* and the *New Criterion*. Ann Hulbert, in the *New Republic,* commented on Morrison's "blissful ignorance of the politicized academic climate" and Bruce Bawer, in the *New Criterion,* called the language of *Playing in the Dark* "tired" and "stultifying" and accused Morrison of having "absolutely nothing original to say."

In spite of such verbal assaults from literary critics, Morrison was clearly committed to developing and playing a more visible role as a social commentator in the 1990s. By the fall of 1992, she had edited and written an introduction to another critical study, a collection of essays with the rather unwieldy title *Race-ing Justice, En-Gendering Power: Essays on Anita Hill, Clarence Thomas and the Construction of Social Reality.* In her stinging introductory essay, Morrison draws a parallel between the character of the "savage cannibal" Friday, subjugated by the shipwrecked sailor Robinson Crusoe in Daniel Defoe's classic novel, and Supreme Court justice Clarence Thomas, who Morrison asserts needed to subjugate his own black identity in order to gain acceptance into white American society.

Both Friday and Clarence Thomas accompany their rescuers into the world of power and salvation. But the problem of rescue still exists: both men, black but unrecognizable at home or away, are condemned first to mimic, then to internalize and adore, but never to utter one single sentence understood to be beneficial to their original culture, whether they are the people who wanted to hurt them or those who loved them to death.

Traveling to an academic conference in the Rioja district of northwest Spain in the spring of 1992, Morrison spoke candidly with a journalist from the English newspaper the *Independent.*

"I am really Chloe Anthony Wofford," she said. "That's who I am. I have been writing under this other person's name. I write some things now as Chloe Wofford, private things. I regret having called myself Toni Morrison when I published my first novel, *The Bluest Eye.*" To her close friends and family members, as well as in her own private thoughts, she may have remained Chloe Wofford, but it was under "this other person's name"—Toni Morrison—that seemingly everyone wanted an opinion from her. She was very much in demand as a public speaker, reading from her novels to standing-room-only crowds, asked to comment on virtually every social and political issue of the 1990s from the rioting that followed the so-called Rodney King trial in Los Angeles to the impact of the rise in teenage pregnancy on the American family.

With the issue of "family values" receiving so much attention during the 1992 presidential election campaign, Morrison was frequently questioned by interviewers as to how she had managed to raise her two sons on her own while working full-time as an editor, teacher, and novelist. Her response was to point out that she had not done it on her own—she had constantly called on her family members for help.

"My little saying is one person cannot raise a child," she said. "Neither can two. You need everybody—you need everybody you know."

In the spring of 1993, Morrison appeared for a one-hour interview on "The Charlie Rose Show," a nationally televised public television program. Midway through the interview Rose, a white North Carolinian, quoted a remark made by the late tennis star Arthur Ashe, who had told Rose shortly before his death that living with AIDS was actually easier than living with racism.

Rose then asked whether Toni Morrison, with all her status as a Pulitzer Prize–winning author and an Ivy League academic, still had the painful experience of the daily encounter with racism.

"Yes, I do, Charlie," she answered, "but, let me tell you, that's the wrong question."

"What's the right question?" he asked.

"How do *you* feel?" she said, explaining that the ramifications of racism should be examined as closely by white Americans as they are by black Americans.

"If you can only be tall because somebody is on their knees, then you have a serious problem," Morrison said. "Don't you understand that the people who do this thing, who practice racism, are bereft? There is something distorted about the psyche. It's a huge waste; it's a corruption, and a distortion. It's like a profound neurosis, that nobody examines for what it is. It feels crazy; it *is* crazy. And it has just as much of a deleterious effect on white people . . . as it does on black people.

"I always knew that I had the moral high-ground, all my life," Morrison told Rose. "I always thought those people who said I couldn't come in the drugstore, and I had to sit in this funny place, and I couldn't go in the park—I thought they knew that I knew that they were inferior to me, morally. I always thought that. And my parents always thought that."

Morrison lecturing at Harvard University in 1990. "She delves into the language itself, a language she wants to liberate from the fetters of racism," said the Nobel Prize committee in announcing her award in 1993. "And she addresses us with the luster of poetry."

She then recounted a painful episode that had happened to her more than a half century earlier in Lorain, Ohio, as an illustration of how virtually every ethnic group learns racism—learns to define itself in opposition to black Americans—upon arrival in the United States.

As a second-grader Chloe Wofford had been an exceptionally good reader, and the teacher would often send new students, poor readers, or immigrant children who did not yet know English well to sit next to her and share her textbook.

One such student was a boy whose family had recently immigrated to Ohio from Italy. This young boy arrived in class without knowing English and was immediately sent to sit with Chloe Wofford. They shared a reader and soon became good friends. He was very bright and she taught him how to read English relatively quickly.

Then one day, about six weeks later, the Italian boy came into class and he would not sit next to Chloe. He would not even speak to her.

"He had learned, in six weeks, not only the word 'nigger' but what that meant, and how disempowering it was for him to be my friend," Morrison recalled.

Now in her early sixties, clearly at the height of her literary career, Morrison was hard at work on her next novel, the third part of the trilogy that had begun with *Beloved* and *Jazz*. This book would take place in the 1970s and 1980s, but flash back to a little-known aspect of 19th-century African-American history, the hundreds of all-black towns that African-Americans had founded immediately after the Civil War. These were not merely black neighborhoods but self-contained townships, with black-operated banks and businesses and schools.

The working title of the novel was *Paradise*. "That's what they thought they were building," Morrison explained.

Asked by Charlie Rose about her work as a professor at Princeton, Morrison made a statement about the field of African-American studies that might very well be applied to her own accomplished body of work.

"If you study the culture and art of African-Americans, you are not studying a regional or minor culture," Morrison said. "What you are studying is America."

The extent of Morrison's study did not go unnoticed by the Nobel Committee of the Swedish

Academy, which awards the Nobel Prize. On October 7, 1993, the academy announced that she was the recipient of the 1993 Nobel Prize in Literature. Toni Morrison "gives life to an essential aspect of American reality" in novels "characterized by visionary force and poetic import," the academy stated. "She delves into the language itself, a language she wants to liberate from the fetters of race. And she addresses us with the luster of poetry."

Morrison became the eighth woman—and the first black woman—to receive the Nobel Prize in Literature, which includes an award of $825,000. "This is palpable tremor of delight for me," she said upon learning of the honor. "It was wholly unexpected and so satisfying. Regardless of what we all say and truly believe about the irrelevances of prizes and their relationship to the real work, nevertheless this is a signal honor for me."

Sixty-two years after being born Chloe Wofford in Lorain, Ohio, Morrison could look back on this crowning achievement and "claim representation in so many areas. I'm a Midwesterner . . . a New Yorker, and a New Jerseyan, and an American, plus I'm an African-American, and a woman. I know it seems like I'm spreading like algae when I put it this way, but I'd like to think of the prize being distributed to these regions and nations and races." ❧

APPENDIX: BOOKS BY TONI MORRISON

1970   *The Bluest Eye*
1973   *Sula*
1977   *Song of Solomon*
1981   *Tar Baby*
1987   *Beloved*
1992   *Jazz; Playing in the Dark: Whiteness and the Literary Imagination*

CHRONOLOGY

——— ❦ ———

1931	Born Chloe Anthony Wofford, February 18 in Lorain, Ohio, the second child of Ramah (Willis) and George Wofford
1949	Graduates from Lorain High School
1953	Graduates from Howard University with B.A. in English; changes her name to Toni during years at Howard
1955	Receives M.A. in English from Cornell University
1955–57	Begins teaching career as instructor of English at Texas Southern University
1957	Returns to Howard University as instructor of English and the humanities
1958	Marries Jamaican architect Harold Morrison
1962	First son, Harold Ford, is born
1965	Divorces Harold Morrison and returns with infant son to Lorain
1965–67	Works as associate editor for a textbook subsidiary of Random House in Syracuse, New York
1966	Second son, Slade Kevin, is born
1967	Becomes senior editor at Random House in New York City
1970	Morrison's first novel, *The Bluest Eye,* is published
1971–72	Becomes associate professor of English at the State University of New York at Purchase
1974	*Sula,* second novel, is published
1975	*Sula* nominated for National Book Award
1976–77	Visiting lecturer at Yale University
1977	*Song of Solomon,* Morrison's third novel, is published by Knopf and wins National Book Critic's Circle Award and the American Academy and Institute of Arts and Letters Award; appointed to National Council on the Arts by President Jimmy Carter
1979	Appointed associate professor at the State University of New York, Purchase; teaches at Bard College
1981	Publishes fourth novel, *Tar Baby;* appears on cover of *Newsweek* magazine
1983	Leaves Random House after twenty years
1984	Named Albert Schweitzer Professor of the Humanities at the State University of New York, Albany
1986	Premiere of first play, *Dreaming Emmett,* at the Marketplace Theater in Albany
1986	Receives the New York State Governor's Art Award
1987	*Beloved,* Morrison's fifth novel, is published

1988	Forty-eight leading black writers and critics write a protest letter to the *New York Times* when *Beloved* does not receive the National Book Award; *Beloved* is awarded the Pulitzer Prize for fiction
1989	Appointed Robert F. Goheen Professor in the Humanities at Princeton University, the first black woman to have an endowed chair at an Ivy League college
1990	Delivers a series of three lectures, part of the William E. Massey, Sr., Lectures in the History of American Civilization, at Harvard University
1992	Publishes *Jazz*, a novel set in Harlem in the 1920s; publishes *Playing in the Dark*, an analysis of the African-American role in American literature, based on the William E. Massey, Sr., lecture series at Harvard; edits and writes introduction to *Race-ing Justice, En-Gendering Power*, a book of essays on the Clarence Thomas hearings.
1993	Wins Nobel Prize in Literature

FURTHER READING

Bloom, Harold, ed. *Toni Morrison*. New York: Chelsea House, 1990.

Evans, Mari, ed. *Black Women Writers, 1950–1980: A Critical Evaluation*. Garden City, NY: Anchor Books, 1984.

Harper, Michael S., and Robert B. Stepto, eds. *Chant of Saints: A Gathering of Afro-American Literature, Art, and Scholarship*. Champaign: University of Illinois Press, 1979.

Hine, Darlene Clark, ed. *Black Women in America: An Historical Encyclopedia*. Vol. 2. Brooklyn, NY: Carlson Publishing, 1993.

Holloway, Karla F., and Stephanie Demetrakopoulos. *New Dimensions of Spirituality: A Biracial and Bicultural Reading of the Novels of Toni Morrison*. Contributions in Women's Studies: No. 84. Westport, CT: Greenwood, 1987.

Jones, Bessie W., and Audrey L. Vinson. *The World of Toni Morrison: Explorations in Literary Criticism*. Dubuque, IA: Kendall-Hunt, 1985.

Lanker, Brian. *I Dream a World: Portraits of Black Women Who Changed America*. Edited by Barbara Summers. New York: Stewart, Tabori & Chang, 1989.

McKay, Nellie Y. *Critical Essays on Toni Morrison*. Boston: G. K. Hall, 1988.

Ruas, Charles. *Conversations with American Writers*. New York: Knopf, 1985.

Smith, Jessie Carney, ed. *Epic Lives: One Hundred Black Women Who Made a Difference*. Detroit, MI: Visible Ink Press, 1993.

INDEX

Albany, New York, 71, 72, 73, 80
Ali, Muhammad, 43
American Academy and Institute of Arts and Letters, 60
Atwood, Margaret, 78

Baldwin, James, 79
Bambara, Toni Cade, 43, 68, 71
Baraka, Amiri, 36
Beloved, 74–81, 84, 88, 94
  critic response, 78–79
  plot, 75–78
  publication, 78
  writing of, 73–78, 84–85
"Bit, the," 77
Black American Literature Forum, 45
Black Book, The (Harris), 53–55, 71, 73
Blackburn, Sara, 50
Black World, 19
Bluest Eye, The, 11–19, 27, 39, 41, 43, 44–46, 50, 86, 91
  critic response, 18–19, 44–45, 50
  plot, 16–18, 38, 42
  publication, 18, 19, 44, 45
  writing of, 11–18, 27, 41, 43, 45
Book-of-the-Month Club, 50, 60
Brooks, Gwendolyn, 15
Brown, Claude, 37
Brown, Sterling A., 31, 33

Carmichael, Stokely, 14, 36–37
Carter, Jimmy, 60
Cavett, Dick, 69
Civil rights movement, 35, 36, 72
Cornell University, 35
Cosby, Bill, 53
Critique: Studies in Modern Fiction, 45
Cullen, Countee, 87

Davis, Angela, 43
Dreaming Emmett, 72–73

Ellington, Duke, 87
Ellison, Ralph, 13, 79

First Congregational Society, 31
Freedmen's Bureau, 31

Gant, Liz, 19
García Márquez, Gabriel, 60
Garner, Margaret, 55, 73–74, 84, 86
Garvey, Marcus, 87
Gordon, Mary, 68
Great Depression, 21, 23, 27, 67

Hansberry, Lorraine, 15
Harlem, New York, 85, 87
Harlem Book of the Dead (Van Der Zee), 85
Harlem Renaissance, 31, 87
Harris, Joel Chandler, 63
Harris, Middleton (Spike), 53, 55, 73
Harvard Advocate, 50
Harvard University, 88
Holt, Rinehart & Winston, 18, 44
Howard, Oliver Otis, 31
Howard University, 12, 14, 29, 31–35, 36, 38
  Players, 33, 34
Hughes, Langston, 87
Hurston, Zora Neale, 15

Jazz, 84–90, 94
  critic response, 88–89
  plot, 86–87
  publication, 88
  writing of, 84–88

Jones, Gayl, 43, 71
Jones, LeRoi. *See* Baraka, Amiri

Kennedy, William, 72
King, Martin Luther, Jr., 14, 35, 36, 72
Klotman, Phyllis R., 45
Knopf, Alfred A., 85
Ku Klux Klan, 22

Leonard, John, 19, 78
Locke, Alain, 31
London Times, 78
Lorain, Ohio, 12, 14, 16, 21, 22, 25, 26, 27, 29, 31, 39, 42, 46, 54, 56, 57, 93, 95
Lorain High School, 29
Los Angeles Times, 78, 89

Manchild in the Promised Land (Brown), 37
Márquez, Gabriel García. *See* García Márquez, Gabriel.
Milkman Dead. See Song of Solomon
Montgomery bus boycott, 35
Morrison, Harold (husband), 37, 38, 39
Morrison, Harold Ford (son), 11, 12, 18, 37, 38, 39, 43, 55, 56, 60, 61, 67
Morrison, Slade (son), 11, 12, 18, 39, 43, 55, 56, 60, 67
Morrison, Toni (Chloe Anthony Wofford)
  appointments and awards, 50, 60, 71, 79–81, 83, 95
  articles and essays, 45, 53, 90–91
  birth, 21
  on black cultural issues, 45, 50, 53–55, 90, 91

changes name, 24, 33, 91
childhood, 12, 21–29, 42
on cover of *Newsweek*, 67–68
editorial career, 11, 18, 41, 43, 44, 53–55, 56, 60, 66, 67, 68, 71, 90, 91
education, 12, 24, 29, 31–35
lectures, 88
marriage, 37, 39
novels, 11–19, 27, 38, 41, 43, 44, 45, 46–51, 55, 57–60, 63–65, 66, 67, 68, 69, 74–78, 81, 84–90, 88–90, 91, 94
plays, 72–73
on racism, 92–93
teaching career, 14, 35, 36, 37, 38, 39, 56, 60, 66, 67, 71, 83, 84, 88, 91
tour of the South, 33–35
wins Nobel Prize, 95
wins Pulitzer Prize, 79

Nation, 50, 89
National Book Award, 50, 79
National Book Critics Circle Award, 60, 79
National Council on the Arts, 60, 69
Native Son (Wright), 60
Naylor, Gloria, 42, 50
New Orleans, 72
Newsweek, 21, 43, 67, 68
New York City, 11, 18, 41, 43, 46, 57, 61, 65, 66, 87
New York State Writers Institute, 72
New York Times, 19, 45, 50, 72, 80
New York Times Book Review, 50, 78, 79, 88
New York Times Magazine, 53, 66, 67
Nobel Prize, 94–95

Oberlin College, 22
Ogunyemi, Chikwenye Okonjo, 45

Ohio, 13, 18, 21, 22, 23, 26, 42, 47, 73, 75, 85, 94

Paradise, 94
Parks, Rosa, 35
Pickering, John, 55
Playing in the Dark: Whiteness and the Literary Imagination, 88–90
critic response, 88, 90
Price, Leontyne, 68
Princeton University, 83–84, 94
Pulitzer Prize, 79, 80

Race-ing Justice, En-Gendering Power: Essays on Anita Hill, Clarence Thomas and the Construction of Social Reality, 90–91
Racism, 14, 21, 23, 24, 25, 26, 33–35, 72–73, 92, 93, 95
Rampersand, Arnold, 83
Random House, 11, 18, 41, 43, 44, 53, 60, 66, 68, 71
Redbook, 50
"Rediscovering Black History," 53
Robeson, Paul, 83–84
Roosevelt, Franklin Delano, 27
Rose, Charlie, 92, 94

Schott, Webster, 68
Slavery, 22, 55, 58, 64, 73–75, 77–78
Smith, Bessie, 87
Song of Solomon, 56, 57–60, 64, 65, 66, 68
critic response, 60
plot, 28, 57–59
publication, 56, 59, 60
writing of, 57, 59
State University of New York, Albany, 71
Student Nonviolent Coordinating Committee (SNCC), 14, 37
Sula, 46–51, 55

critic response, 50–51, 55
plot, 47–49
publication, 50
writing of, 46
Syracuse, New York, 11, 13, 19, 41, 42, 43

Tallchief, Maria, 27
Tar Baby, 63–65, 67, 68, 69
critic response, 68–69
legend behind, 63, 64
plot, 64–65
publication, 64, 65
writing of, 64–65
Texas Southern University, 35
They Came Before Columbus (Van Sertima), 71
Till, Emmett, 72–73

Uncle Remus, 63
Underground Railroad, 22

Van Der Zee, James, 85
Van Sertima, Ivan, 71
"Visit to the Slave Mother Who Killed Her Child, A," 73–74

Walker, Alice, 50
Washington Book World, 68
Washington, D.C., 12, 29, 31, 34
West, Cornell, 83
Willis, John Solomon (grandfather), 21, 22, 34, 35
Wofford, Chloe Anthony. *See* Morrison, Toni.
Wofford, George (father), 21, 23, 24, 25, 27, 28, 29, 34, 39, 56, 57, 66
Wofford, Ramah Willis (mother), 21, 24, 26, 27, 28, 29, 34, 39, 46
Women's liberation movement, 47

Yale University, 56, 60, 66
Young, Andrew, 36, 43

PICTURE CREDITS

———— ❧ ————

DOUGLAS CENTURY was born and raised in Canada and graduated from Princeton University with a degree in English and creative writing. He has published fiction and nonfiction in a number of newspapers and magazines including the *Village Voice*, *New York Newsday*, *Midstream*, and *Forward*. He lives in New York City and is currently working on a novel and an original screenplay.

NATHAN IRVIN HUGGINS, one of America's leading scholars in the field of black studies, helped select the titles for the BLACK AMERICANS OF ACHIEVEMENT series, for which he also served as senior consulting editor. He was the W.E.B. Du Bois Professor of History and of Afro-American Studies at Harvard University and the director of the W.E.B. Du Bois Institute for Afro-American Research at Harvard. He received his doctorate from Harvard in 1962 and returned there as a professor in 1980 after teaching at Columbia University, the University of Massachusetts, Lake Forest College, and the California State University, Long Beach. He was the author of four books and dozens of articles, including *Black Odyssey: The Afro-American Ordeal in Slavery*, *The Harlem Renaissance*, and *Slave and Citizen: The Life of Frederick Douglass*, and was associated with the Children's Television Workshop, National Public Radio, the Boston Athenaeum, the Museum of Afro-American History, the Howard Thurman Educational Trust, and Upward Bound. Professor Huggins died in 1989, at the age of 62, in Cambridge, Massachusetts.